"NO WEAPON FORMED AGAINST THEE SHALL PROSPER"

Shelley,
A true Worshipper,
worships Him in
spirit and in truth.
You are a blessing
to the Kingdom of God!

love in Christ
Margaret Prince

"NO WEAPON FORMED AGAINST THEE SHALL PROSPER"

BY
MARGARET MARIE M.S., C.R.C.

CREDITS

Work edited by Carol Roman
Work Co-edited, reviewed, and formatted by Fluid K.® Webmaster@Fluidk.zzn.com
Layout ideas, (headers and photos) by boyimlost62@yahoo.com
Additional layout ideas and back cover photo by Tacogurl†
Cover Design Stephen Lisi

Overcomer Publishing
margemariem@excite.com

*credit: **Chapter 1**, Cycles of Abuse borrowed from the works organized by the
Domestic Abuse Intervention Project, 208 West Fourth Street, Duluth, Minnesota 65804
(free literature).

*credit: **Chapter 8**, Abuse Inventory Checklists were extracted from Free Yourself from
an Abusive Relationship (seven steps to getting free) by Andrea Lissette, Hunter House,
Almeda, Ca. 2000.

*credit: **Conclusion**, The Personal Safety Plan, was extracted directly from the New
York State Office for the Prevention of Domestic Violence, "Finding Safety and Support
/Domestic Violence", all rights reserved, Capital View Office Park, 52 Washington
Street, Rensselaer, New York. 12144, copyright 1996, 2000, (NYSOPDV-free literature).

DEDICATION AND
EXPRESSIONS OF GRATITUDE

I Corinthians 13: 1-8

"Though I speak with the tongues of men and of angels, and have not love, I am become as sounding brass or a tinkling cymbal. And though I have the gift of prophecy, and understand all mysteries and all knowledge, and though I have all faith, so that I could remove mountains, and have not love, I am nothing. And though I bestow all my goods to feed the poor, and though I give my body to be burned, and have not love, it profiteth me nothing. Love suffereth long and is kind; love envieth not; love vaunteth not itself, is not puffed up, doth not behave itself unseemly, seeketh not her own, is not easily provoked, thinketh no evil; rejoiceth not in iniquity but rejoiceth in the truth, beareth all things, believeth all things, hopeth all things, endureth all things. Love NEVER fails…"

First, I would like to give all glory to my God, and thank Him for what He has done in my life.

This book is dedicated primarily to my spiritual mother, Joanne Servello. Joanne every bit reflects what God's word says about love. The mark of God on her life and relentless love that she sheds abroad to others around her, is the reason that I am able to fulfill the call of God that is on my life.

I know that it is really God that makes all things possible, but the body of Christ need each other in order to have the strength to continue to carry on the good fight, and respond well while doing so. Thank you, Joanne, for your obedience and persistent love to us! My whole family LOVES you dearly.

A special thank you to Judy Pucillo for being there for me so that I would not have to stand alone and for her obedience to God to flow in her gifting of deliverance. Thanks, to Mom, my sister, brother, and sister-in-law for all the support, love and safe haven during difficult times.

I cannot forget to mention my dear friend, Carleen Taylor. My thankful heart goes out to Carleen's faithful and unconditional acceptance and love. No matter how adverse situations got, Carleen was there for the children and I. Thank you, Carleen. I will love you forever.

Last, but first in God's eyes, I need to thank my courageous children who God has great plans for.

I wish more than anything that I could reach out and take back every pain, disappointment, fear, frustration, provocation, bit of anger and trauma that was afflicted upon you. I do so love each creative hair on your heads and special personality that each of you has. Though I'm still not clear on why we endure some things, the one thing I am clear on is that God has taught each one of us how to be victorious despite the odds being stacked against us.

Each one of you is very valuable and special to God and me. God knew each of you when you were just seeds in my womb. I cannot take any blame, nor can I take any credit for the unique individuals that you are.

God made you the way you are and He wants you to tap into the vision that He has had for each of you from the beginning of your creation. I am truly sorry for the abuse that you had to endure, and for those who don't know how to say that they are sorry, or who are gone and simply will never say that they are sorry: I stand in the gap for them, that you each come to know how important it is to forgive all those who have hurt you in your lives. Release those that have hurt you and set yourselves free. Thank you for the special people that you are and for just being yourselves. I love you all very much, and I always will.

Other special thanks:

Thank you, Carol Roman, for your unconditional acceptance shown toward the creation of this book. Thank you for your willing, obedient and prayerful attitude while editing this work. I believe that God knit us together years ago it is sweet how much God loves us through special people that He designs in our paths.

I would also like to especially thank the "pioneer women" who were the financial and physical supports that provided supervised visitations that were court mandated during a very difficult and abusive court battle. This is the kind of courage that revival springs out of. Our many thanks to:

Michelle Bennett

Nancy Choquette

Sue Fikes

Diane Gimelli

Dena Huff, domestic violence program (also Wendy, Jackie, and Connie from the same program)

Carol Ann Kovak

Sue MacDonald

Dee Owens

Carleen Taylor

I wish much love and blessings of God upon each of their lives and their family's lives. You are all truly history makers!

A special thanks goes out to Debbie Koenig and her family. The physical, financial, and emotional support that they provided myself, and my family throughout the years was essential to our survival.

I would also like to thank my Pastor and his wife for being such great leaders and showing relentless love for my family. Thank you, Pastor for critiquing my book, your suggestions were well taken and my hope is that through this book, many people will be saved, their lives set free from bondage. Thanks to my worship leader for allowing me to find my way out of the pit of violence as a vessel of worship for the nine years that I was privileged to be a part of the worship team at Mt. Zion. Those were breakthrough years for me, and I would not be where I am today had I not found God in worship and praise.

A special thanks to all our great pastors and elders at Mt. Zion I am so glad to have my family at Mt. Zion and such a blessed church home.

In the church there are too many people to name who prayed, offered support, words of encouragement, physical assistance, needed items, clothes, gifts to the children Thank you all. A special thanks to my country neighbor who was a watchdog for my house as I was under great pressure during the 2-year court battle, thanks for praying Barb.

PROLOGUE

It was dark, and as I ran it was difficult to know whether the chill I felt was the sweat that poured off my brow or if my blood had actually begun to run cold inside of me. I found it so impossible to discern where I was going or even why I was running in the dark.

At first, I thought I had entered an un-kept field of hay, but it became increasingly obscure each time I lifted a foot to take another step. It was as if something was holding me back- grabbing, not only my feet, but my legs were becoming entangled as well. I looked down at the ground. Reaching to feel my legs, I could barely make out what looked like razor sharp tendrils that wrapped around my ankles and knees. Eventually, my steps were immobilized and I fell on my face.

As I gasped for breath, I saw the moon's reflection upon the villain that held me tight, entrapped. It was belladonna, a solanaceous herb that appears quite lovely with it's delicate, entwining tendrils and which displays a purplish blossom. Silly- what does this mean? A field of nightshade ensnared me. It sounds quite harmless, but oh, how deadly.

I awoke in a cold sweat. Why was I so frightened? More than a dream, this sense of entrapment and being immobilized loomed over me even after I awoke. Was this a glimpse of something yet to come? Could this entrapment be avoided, averted or prayed away? Had decisions already been made in my life that would result in leaving me trapped somehow? This seemed so very real to me.

The questions I had about this dream grew to haunt me for the next 16 years. I had the dream before I was married to my second husband. You see, I wanted to be careful about who I married, as my first marriage was a disaster.

CHAPTER 1

WAKE UP CALL

It had been two or three days since my second husband had come home. This pattern had begun to repeat itself lately. He would disappear and the children and I would not see him or have a clue where he was for one to three days. In hindsight, I remember the feeling of a war going on inside of me and I know the children must have had these same nagging feelings. It was so peaceful without him. No one was being belittled, screamed at, or in the line of fire of flying objects. Yet, we could not really enjoy the true value of that peace because in reality, we all knew that at any moment, he might come slamming in the door, swearing and intimidating everyone so that no one asked him where he had been. It always seemed like he made up for "lost time " to abuse us all.

Slam! The kids and I were in the kitchen. My son, who was about five years old, was at the table. My daughter who was about three years old, was standing by me at the sink, and, by the grace of God, my oldest son happened to be at a friend's house.

There he was, big as life, very drunk and likened to a maniacal attitude. Adrenalin was coursing through our bodies. As usual, our hearts

1

were beating too fast to breathe comfortably so our eyes watched with great expectancy to see what was going to happen next. The abuser began to scream. It was unclear what the problem was-as always, there did not need to be a problem. He picked up a cast iron kickstand that was broken and recklessly hurled it in my direction. This happened so fast. The kickstand flew with great force until it penetrated the cupboard under the sink. It had missed me, but when I looked down to where my three year old was standing, I saw with horror that the penetration of this iron missed my daughter's head by two inches. This was enough! In terror, I picked my daughter up in my arms, grabbed for my son's hand and ran out the kitchen door with these panicking children. As I took the second step out of the kitchen door, I felt the plate glass door shattering over our heads. I continued to run as the abuser's screams turned to threats-"I'll kill you if you leave." I continued to run. Picking glass off the children so they would not be cut, I lost contact with my son's hand. At this point, my son was screaming out of control. I yelled to my son, "Come with me! We have to go!" We heard the screams of our abuser coming closer. He was back on trail only now with a loaded shotgun. I went back to get my son and the abuser grabbed his hand just as I got to him. I was terrified that the abuser would get my daughter as well. As I was thinking of what I should do next, the abuser put my son into the car; my poor son was kicking and screaming. I knew that we were all at risk of being shot. So, I turned and began to run away. I ran thinking I will get help-I must get help. As I ran, I saw the face of my son screaming. His little face pressed against the window of the car. The drunken abuser tore off down the road with the shotgun and my precious little son screaming "Mommy".

I only wish that this memory could fade from my mind. I was hysterical at this point. I kept thinking my God, my God! Please send your angels to help my son. I ran to the next-door neighbor's house but there was no one home. I then ran to the next house and by now-I was hyperventilating. I saw a face in the window and I thought there is someone to help us! The only problem was that I was having a hard time speaking. I tried to speak but it was hard to get air to do it. I managed to spit out "Call the troopers. Please-right away-my son's life is in danger and maybe ours as well." I spoke to the troopers on the phone; hearing them on the other end of the line brought me to my senses. "I have to get help for my son. His father is drunk and out of control. He abducted my son with a shotgun. Please, you have to save my son. He is in great danger."

The terror had just begun for my son. His father had driven like a maniac to his brother-in-law's house and he tore into the field with the car and began doing 360's. He then took my son out of the car and into his sister's house. He then began to rail uncontrollably and during a dispute with his brother-in-law, who may have been trying to calm him down, the abuser discharged the shotgun once or twice. By the grace of God no one was hurt or killed by the discharge. The troopers arrived on the scene and arrested the abuser for reckless endangerment, resisting arrest. This was only one of many arrest tirades. He was facing up to 25 years in prison. My son was safe but very emotionally scarred.

The following information was borrowed from works organized by the Domestic Abuse Intervention Project, 208 West Fourth Street, Duluth, Minnesota 65804 and embellished upon by my own personal experience, with permission as public knowledge to educate those who are in need.

CYCLES OF ABUSE

Domestic violence is defined as a pattern of intimidating, manipulative behavior with the intent to forcibly establish and maintain power and control over a victim. In most cases of domestic violence, it has been realized that the majority, or 95% of cases; involve men abusing women. For the express purpose of clarity, these writings will come from the perspective of men abusing women. However, it is a fact that 5% of the population who are abused, are of male gender.

Here are some points that express the goals of abuse:

***Abuse is the abuser meeting his needs at the expense of his children and his significant other, or his victims-by using actions, words, or attitudes that hurt, threaten, or humiliate them.

***Abuse is trying to meet or match the abuser's picture of how things should be.

***Abuse is attempting to control others by being out of control.

***Abuse is making someone else feel bad in order for the abuser to feel good (of course it is usually counterproductive).

In the cycle of abuse, power and control can be manifested through various means such as:

5

Physical Abuse

- Shoving, poking, pushing, hitting, punching, kicking, slapping, choking, pulling hair, grabbing, pinching, using a weapon against her, beating, throwing her down to floor or into walls, twisting her arms, tripping, biting, burning, etc.

Emotional Abuse

- Putting her down or making her feel bad about herself, calling her names, making her think she's crazy, playing mind games, lying about an incident that the abused was a direct witness to, denying what is true, isolation, controlling what she does, who she sees and talks to and where she goes.

Intimidation (This can occur through physical, emotional, sexual, spiritual, or other means of abuse)

- Putting her in fear by: using looks, actions, loud voice, smashing objects.
- Destroying her property.

- Calling to harass her on the telephone while he is away.

- Killing household pets, or threatening to.

- Making and / or carrying out threats to do something to hurt her or the children emotionally.

- Threaten to take the children or commit suicide.

- Report her to welfare.

Using Male Privilege: (This can also be a form of spiritual abuse)

- Treating the victim like a servant.

- Making all the "big" decisions, act like the "master of the castle".

- Using the bible in a twisted way to say that the man is the head of the family, (the man is supposed to love his wife like Christ loves His church).

- Forcing her to do immoral acts against her will.

- Acting in ways that are against what she believes.

- Spiritually degrading the victim if she wants to stand against the violence saying, "What therefore God has joined together, let no man put asunder" (Matthew 19:6).

I'll talk more about all of these things in later chapters.

Using Children

- Abusers use the children to make the victim feel guilty.

- Children are used as pawns to give messages to the women.

- They (the abusers) use visitation as a way to harass the women and the children and to gain access to the family.

- The abusers use children to force reconciliation with his victims in order to perpetuate the cycle of abuse.

Economic Abuse

- The abuser will try to keep the victim from getting or keeping a job. If she has a job he may threaten to come to work and denigrate her to her boss with slander, accuse her of having affairs.

- Misappropriate the use of her funds.

- Refusing to give her money for what she needs.

- Making her ask for money and then belittle her.

8

- Ruling absolutely over all spending in the household.
- Taking her money against her will, having tantrums and make threats in order to get money for his own pleasure.
- Riding "guns" over everything in the house, i.e. who ate the food?
- Not allowing the family to have what they need.
- Making money but withhold any money for the upkeep of the family.
- Deceptive practices with intent to rob the victim in any way financially without her knowledge.

Sexual Abuse

Abusers…

- Make the victim do sexual things against her will.
- Physically attack the sexual parts of her body.
- Treat the victim like a sex object.
- Rape the victim.
- Force the victim to interact sexually in a way that she feels dehumanized.

- The abuser makes fun of the victim's abilities to gratify him or threatens to go elsewhere for his gratification.

- Takes naked pictures of the victim against her will.

- The abuser has numerous affairs without remorse and expects the abused victim to accept his behavior.

Now that you have a general understanding of what constitutes abuse, here are the phases that partners in an abusive relationship go through as they perpetuate the abusive lifestyle.

Phase I:

Tension Building

In the beginning of most relationships, violence is rarely shown. The relationship is often one of infatuation or based on pure lust. During this time, there is a lack of stress between partners and positive behavior is shown. This is a time when each partner is on his or her best behavior. The chance of the relationship ending is high if violence occurs at this point.

As the relationship continues, the demands increase along with the stress. There is an increase in aggressive behavior, usually toward objects rather than the partner. For example, punching doors, throwing objects, etc.

The abusive behavior is reinforced by the abuser's release of tension following the violence.

The violence moves from objects to the partner and there may be an increase in verbal abuse as well as physical abuse. It may be one or the other at a traumatic level, not to exclude those victims that experience various types of abusive experiences, i.e. destruction of large proportions, or emotional abuse through verbal battering at a higher level, etc.

The victim or partner may alter her behavior to try to stop the violence, for example, attempting to keep the house cleaner, the children quieter, staying home more often, etc.

The verbal and physical abuse continues. The victim or partner may withdraw and feel responsible for the abuse.

The abuser may become obsessively jealous and try to control most of the victim or partner's life, i.e. dictating where the victim or partner will go, with whom, and may even go as far as dictating how the victim will dress.

The abuser may try to isolate the victim or partner, saying, "If you loved me you would not need other people," or, "Now that we are married, your place is with me!" Sometimes the isolation is more indirect in that the abuser will simply display such tantrum behavior every time the victim tries to spend time away from home that the victim learns that it is safer and more peaceful to submit to the abuser's wishes not to interact with others.

The tension-building phase differs among families in severity and length of time of the development of their own personal tension.

Phase II:

The Acute Battering Incident

In this phase, there may be an actual feeling of release from the built-up stress and tension following the violence.

The abuser makes a choice about his violence. For example, he decides the time and place for the episode, makes a conscious choice on which part of the body to hit and whether it will be done with a fist or an open hand, or he may decide, "I am losing control and something is going to get smashed". He may fix on something to smash that will hurt the victim since this is the means to regain his power and control as discussed earlier. This kind of incident, **however played out, usually warrants law enforcement to become involved.** (As an added note, a criminal act has been committed and there is an opportunity to press charges against the abuser. Often women are afraid to do so as their abuser will usually be released the next day and come back to them with vengeance. We will take baby steps through all of the issues in these writings.)

As a result of the abuse, the pent up stress and tension have been eliminated. Therefore, the abuser often appears calm and relaxed when police arrive. The victim or partner, on the other hand, may appear confused or hysterical from the episode.

Phase III:

The Calm Phase

This phase is characterized by a calm, non-violent or loving period after an abusive episode.

For purely manipulative reasons, the abuser may take some responsibility for his behavior thus giving the victim or partner hope for change. The abuser may beg for forgiveness, promise not to do it again, promise to get help, act as if nothing happened, give gifts, flowers and so on to make it up to the victim. There may even be tears of great sorrow.

If there is no intervention and the relationship continues, there is a high possibility the **<u>violence will escalate and the severity will increase.</u>**

Unless the abuser receives help in learning appropriate methods of dealing with stress and anger, this phase will not last. The stress and tension will again begin to increase and the cycle will repeat itself over and over again.

As you read so many times, children who grow up in an abusive environment either grow up to marry an abusive spouse, or worse, they themselves fall victim to the vicious cycle of abuse and become abusive to those who are closest to them.

Sadly enough, I fit the textbook example of many of these convictions. From a very small child, I was abused physically, emotionally, verbally, and sexually. When I was at the age of 11 years, my mother broke free of the abusive hold my father had on her. With the support of the Department of Social Services, mom made a very painful decision to place myself, and my four siblings in foster care homes. After the initial break from domestic violence, my three brothers were placed into three separate homes. At first I had thought that mercy was upon me because my sister and I were the only 2 of the five children that stayed together and lived in the same foster home. Unfortunately, what I had initially thought would be merciful for my sister and I, soon turned into an emotional "roller coaster" which left scars on both of us for the rest of our lives.

As fate would have it, the foster father was more abusive than my alcoholic natural father. The major difference between the two was that my foster father was being paid a decent wage by the county to abuse other people's children.

I'm not writing this book to prey on emotions. My intent is to paint a brief history of someone like me who happened to survive a rough childhood only to perpetuate that misery in adulthood and clearly state in these writings some principle truths I've come to know-however long it may have taken me! Ultimately, it is a desire of mine to <u>help</u> <u>others</u> who find themselves on the same "roller coaster" ride that I was on. It is my desire to help them find a **<u>safe</u>** way off the roller coaster before their traumatized lives end in destruction- just as a roller coaster that has no controls winds recklessly until it will also meet certain destruction.

I use the roller coaster example because it works to demonstrate very well some of what I was feeling when I lived in the abused lifestyle. For example, no one in their right mind would jump off a roller coaster, would they? Let's just say you thought the ride looked like something you might want to do. You make a choice to get on the ride. Suddenly, you realize this is too scary. Do you jump off? No! As scary (maybe even terrifying) as the ride may be you don't feel like you have a choice. You will surely be killed if you jump. Perhaps you have found yourself on this ride with children. Now you are responsible for their little lives. You may say to yourself, "what was I thinking? How did we even get on this ride?" Surely you can't endanger their lives any more than you feel you already have. Now little ones can be destroyed if you jump when the ride gets unbearable. So what do you do? The truth is, you remain frozen or immobilized on the treacherous ride, hoping over each bend or rise for a way out that is **safe**- **safe** for your children, and **safe** for you.

As you may have guessed at this point, my first husband was an abuser. I was with him for 11 years. He too was an alcoholic and was abusive to my son and I. In later chapters, I will address the spiritual impact such a lifestyle holds upon a family providing no spiritual authority is exercised against such things. I will teach you about how humans have a spiritual side and the importance of realizing that you can stop blaming yourself for everything that has brought you to this point.

In this chapter, I want to draw your attention to the heart of this book. Is there someone who is reading this book and asking the questions, "Can I get out of this situation? Will I be strong enough to fight in the beaten down state that I'm in? He says he loves me. Even if I wanted to get out of this, how can I withstand the pain? My heart is so broken right now. I don't believe I can take any more pain and rejection." I'm here to tell you there is hope. You can and will get through this despite how you feel.

You begin by taking baby steps. The first courageous step is beyond asking "how" to do it. The real key decision is to tell yourself the truth, which is, "My life and my children's lives are valuable and they are being destroyed. I have no choice but to say to myself, 'I choose not to live this way anymore,'" and don't change your mind.

Once this decision has been made, you need to stand strong without wavering, and make no more excuses. The circle or cycle of abuse has to be broken by your decision not to let it go on anymore.

Let's face it. No one wants to be abused unless there are serious mental, emotional, and or spiritual problems. No one wants to be used, mistreated, terrorized, or put down physically, mentally, emotionally, spiritually-or any other way.

It's interesting, how an abusive lifestyle can cause victims to survive day to day on automatic pilot in a warped place-without giving any real thought or information to themselves about their situation. The victim reacts this way because it is a natural defense mechanism, which enables them to survive. The victim is desensitized from the reality of what is happening.

Now relax. I know exactly what you are feeling right now-"Stuff it, lady! I am not the one who is doing anything wrong. I am a victim." I hear what you are saying. My only response to this is that I am asking you to commit to make the conscious decision not to live like this. Am I asking you to get out immediately? **Only if it is safe and it is possible**. In reality, most women have to brave the decision and establish it in their mind (heart) first. Then they can actually make a plan and take action.

The first rule is "BE SAFE". Most often, the person who has lived the abuse as a victim has a pretty fair understanding of how safe she is, given her own individual circumstances. This may not be true in every case, such as cases where emotional damage has led to mental instability.

Before you leave, ask yourself, " Do I have the strength to stay out of this situation and not cave in to the manipulative controlling attitudes that my abuser will impose on me and the children?"(If there are any children). "ARE WE SAFE?"

I am NOT saying these things to discourage the victim of abuse from leaving this situation. Realize that you will be in for a fight to stay away from the abuser. This is part of the WAKE UP CALL to come to the knowledge that you can be free if you are ready to make that decision.

Please understand that God's word says, "You shall know the truth, and the truth will set you free." (John 8:32) Sometimes the truth is hard to see. I know, I have been there.

Let's get back to my decision whether to marry my second husband. Sixteen years ago, I had decided to remarry a man who was supposed to be studying to be a minister. We dated for two years before marrying. I thought, "I have to be safe with him. He's a student of the ministry." Guess again! This husband was physically, emotionally, verbally, and sexually abusive to me.

So, as some people say, what's the matter lady? Have you got rocks for brains? Well, I know that many women who have fallen prey to a manipulative, controlling attitude have asked themselves the same question.

Living this type of lifestyle is not only dangerous but could even be deadly, but also the weight of emotional damage is unbearable at times. Abused women may not know how to be loved by a man or receive love from anyone. The humiliation and daily degradation that the victim of abuse sustains causes them depressive blows to who they are. This adds to their self-rejection. Of course, the abusers know this all too well and use every tactic possible to continue to toy with their victim and keep them in a state of immobility.

The most important point to remember from this chapter is **"BE SAFE!!!!"** If the daily roller coaster ride you are on is getting scarier than you can handle, make a conscious decision to get out. Find people that can help and support you. Make a plan and begin to fix your thoughts on freedom. Like Lot's wife who was turned into a pillar of salt, don't look back at the situation. Make a courageous decision not to live like that anymore. When you know the time is right to carry out what you have decided, take action. Stay in strong company for support and advocacy and get free.

Take a moment to quietly say this prayer with me:

Thank you lord, for forgiving me of all sin.

Thank you for the strength that you give to me.

Your word says I can do all things through Christ who strengthens me. (Philippians 4:13)

Thank you for loving me, for helping me to make good decisions, and for giving me a clear vision to be free from this unsafe situation.

Thank you for renewed hope. Thank you for safety!

In Jesus name ...Amen

CHAPTER 2

AS A MAN THINKETH IN HIS HEART, SO IS HE

Why is there such a need to decide in our hearts, or our minds, what we need to do? That's simple. The abuser has already decided that his major passion is to control his victim. The abuser's intent, whether carefully calculated or impulsively done, is to immobilize the victim and to maintain the state of mind that the victim of abuse is in.

The predominant weapon that the abuser uses over the victim is <u>FEAR.</u> This is why so many abusive partners resent it when they see their victims becoming more self-reliant, going to school or joining any kind of social group-church related or otherwise. In some cases the abusive partner does not want the victim working a job. (In other cases, such as mine, they gladly have the victim working several jobs while they sit home and drink or drug the money away). When challenged, the abusive partner begins to fear that he is losing his grip on the victim when he sees these or other changes from the usual pattern of blind submission. The abuser does not take this very lightly. Usually, such suspicions by the abusers will actually prompt a battering or rage of tyranny. The purpose for this explosive reaction is to put the victim back into the immobile state by inducing fear in the victim and especially the children (if there are children). In addition, the abuser also hopes to browbeat the victim into feeling <u>GUILT</u> in an attempt to force the victim back into submission. I would like to expand on guilt for a moment.

According to Louis O. Caldwell, if we seek to understand the nature of guilt, it may be helpful to classify two kinds of guilt:

1. <u>Guilt as a moral condition, and</u>

2. <u>Guilt as a personality disorder.</u>

In consideration of the moral condition, the bible says that "None is righteous, no, not one."(Romans 3:10) That is to say, we have all fallen short of God's glory, His standard of living, and His moral law. The guilt is rooted from that violation of God's moral law and our alienation from God because of sin in our lives.

In review of the personality disturbance due to a sense of guilt, we see that it goes beyond our moral condition to moral awareness, which has origin in our conscience. Moral awareness goes all the way back to Adam and Eve[1] when they hid from God's presence due to disobedience to Him. Stay with me

---

[1]"And they heard the voice of the Lord God walking in the garden in the cool of the day, and Adam and his wife hid themselves from the presence of the Lord God among the trees of the garden..." (Genesis 3:8)

now! Although the word conscience does not appear in the Old Testament, the concept is present and expressed by the word "heart".

That brings us back to my original question-why is there such a need for us to decide in our hearts? Proverbs 23:7 tells us "For as a man thinketh in his heart, so is he. Eat and drink, saith he to thee, but his heart is not with thee." A victim can be so oppressed with guilt that it becomes a way of life or a personality disturbance that impacts on decisions that are made daily. If the abuser can get the victim to be in the downtrodden state of "immobility" or to be a prisoner in the heart, then she is immobile or imprisoned. You may have heard the expression; "There are some prisoners in an actual prison with bars and walls that are freer than some who are prisoners of the heart or mind." In summation, one of the greatest manipulative efforts of any abuser is to keep his victim(s) feeling GUILTY! "Guilty for what?" you may ask. Anything and everything; is your fault! The most unnatural part of this whole, unnatural way of life is that the abuser will even convince the victim that it is her fault that he physically, emotionally, mentally, or sexually abuses her. Guilt and condemnation are favorite tools of the abuser.

I would like to borrow some more noted words of Louis O. Caldwell as he describes "conscience", or heart, in a very clear manner. The bible indicates in Romans 2:14-15, "For when the Gentiles which

have not the law, do by nature the things contained
in the law, these, having not the law, are a law unto
themselves...which shew the work of the law
written in their hearts, their conscience also bearing
witness, and their thoughts- the meanwhile accusing
or excusing one another..." So, although the
conscience or heart may be influenced by our
environment-however good or bad it may be (i.e.
abusive home, education, ethnic groups, socio-
economic status, habits, or vocational background,
etc.)-It is not the result of any of these factors
solely.

Our conscience or heart functions in three ways:

1. It urges us to do what we know is right
   and restrains us from doing what is
   wrong.

2. It acts as the standard by which we make
   our moral evaluation.

3. It passes judgment on our own actions,
   expressing itself in our personality.

Wrong motives, choices, and deeds result in
inner disturbances such as shame, distress, remorse,
discouragement, and depression. In other words,
wrong motives, choices, and actions can open doors
to deeper bondages. We will discuss this more in
depth in later chapters. Caldwell says that right
behavior brings its own reward of conscience or
heart such as inner peace, and a sense of divine
social and personal approval. Why do people who

have fallen victim to a lifestyle of abuse know what is right to do yet they do what is wrong? The person's conscience or heart has lost health and balance. It has become perverted by the abuse and from believing all the lies that go with it. (Such as denial and disassociation, (See chapter 3 for more discussion on these personality problems). A conscience can also become calloused or dead. This is the worse state of all, as the dulled conscience is the result of repeated, willful, conscious wrongdoing, or in essence, <u>SIN.</u>

The most difficult realization that I had to make when God revealed this to me, was–wretched victim of abuse that I was–I had fallen into sin. I was in sin as a result of a dulled conscience (heart). This was not easy to accept and I cried many tears. The very thought that I had allowed myself to get to this state bothered me. Without the support and assistance from <u>healthy</u> friends, much prayer, and the everlasting love and patience from my Father God, I probably would not have been victorious. The sovereign hand of God touched me and set me free from the "victim mentality" that I had mistakenly thought was "normal" for me. I do not think in my heart that I am a victim, so therefore I have made a good decision that tells me <u>I AM NOT A VICTIM</u>! We need to know what Jesus did for us on the cross.

You may say, "But I am still a victim!" Victim or not (I will talk more about this in the next chapter) it is important to know that God loves you just the way you are and His patience endures forever. God wants us to think in our hearts the way He thinks of us. We are His righteousness and His love is sure to carry us where we need to go if we look to His strength, His will, and to what ONLY HE can do in our lives.

Please take a moment to quietly say this prayer with me:

Thank You, Lord, that I am your righteousness and that You love me no matter what I have done or where I am.

Help me to think of myself the way You think of me.

Help me to see myself as special, because that is how You see me.

Help me to know in my heart that You have a special purpose for my life.

Thank You for the strength that I need and forgive me of things that are in my heart that do not belong there.

Please give me a fresh start. Purify my heart and draw me by Your Spirit to a place where I can see myself with the same love and beauty that you see in me.

Thank You for renewing my mind and heart with the truth which will set me free.

I ask these things in Jesus name.   *AMEN*

CHAPTER 3

THE VICTIM

In Webster's dictionary, the definition of the word "victim" is a person who suffers from a destructive or injurious action or agency; an accident victim, etc., or a person who is deceived or cheated, or a person being sacrificed as in religious rites. The next word listed in alphabetical order is "victor". The definition of victor reads: a person who has overcome or defeated an adversary, or a winner in a struggle or a contest. As I read these definitions, I thought how interesting it was that in my life, Jesus was both the victim and the victor for me.

In this chapter, I want to share some of my own testimony from life experiences that first ingrained the "victim" mentality in me, and how I came to realize that Jesus became the victim for me so that through Him I am now a "VICTOR".

Throughout the course of our lives, most of us are met with various circumstances, due to decisions we make or through no fault of our own, in which we may fall victim to an event that causes us to suffer pain. The key focus here is: What is the victim's reaction to this pain and suffering? Some people become bitter, some stronger willed, and some rise above the pressure they experience through the negative event. Those who rise above are considered overcomers because they defeated their adversary by making the choice to be a victor despite the circumstances. There are others that buckle under the pressure and develop unhealthy thinking, as discussed in the previous chapter, which leads to the "victim" mentality.

Listen for a moment and allow me to share a bit of my own life to demonstrate some of the steps that God has brought me through. God's mercy grabbed hold of the events in my life that the devil had tried to use to destroy me. The Lord made good come out of my life, good that can be shared with others to set them free.

MEMORIES AS A VICTIM

My early memories are painful and filled with insecurity. I was fed with more than the average negative messages by my natural father, who was alcoholic and abusive to my mother and my three brothers, sister and I. The earliest memory of my father hitting me was probably about three years old. My father hit me with such force in the side of the head that I remember flying into the wall underneath the kitchen table. I immediately kept my shelter there between the barricade of the kitchen chair and table legs so that my drunken father could not reach me. He tried to reach me until he lost his focus (because he was too drunk) and then he left me alone. I remember hiding under chairs, tables, beds, and sometimes in the barn. This became routine for all of us.

I was put in a foster home at the age of 11 years old, where I remained for six years. During that six-year period, I witnessed countless brutal beatings of many children that came in and out of the foster home. Many of these children had come from the roots of neglect and abuse already. For some amazing reason, the first time my foster father raised his fist to hit me; I stepped into his face and said, "If you ever lay a hand on me or my sister, I will report you to the police."(I was 11 years old). He never physically beat us, but the emotional, verbal, and psychological abuse was overwhelming. My sister and I cleaned and cooked; we were basically "workhorses" in the house for as many as ten children at a time. Children would constantly come and go from this foster home. When we finished cleaning, ironing and doing the barn-work, our foster father would find work for us to do because in his opinion, we had no right to have fun. One time he made us harvest a field of mustard (ragweed) with our bare hands just to keep us busy. Children in domestic violence situations do not have the luxury of being children or developmentally coming alive the way a normal child in a safe home does.

We lived down the road from a country church and one day a man came to the foster home and invited us to come to his church. When the foster father was not home, my foster mother was a lot nicer, and she would let us go. I began to attend church every Sunday and one week a missionary from China was visiting the church. She told us how people in China had to hide their belief in Christ. God used this missionary to lead me to the His saving knowledge. She prayed with me and I asked God to forgive me of my sins and for Jesus to come into my heart and be Lord of my life. I was 16 years old. Oh, what a relief it was to talk to Jesus, to feel His strength upon my life and to know that I was no longer alone in this situation.

My newfound faith angered my foster father. He told me that I was forbidden to read the bible and that I could not go to church anymore. I remember the feeling of being a victim. Unfortunately, instead of crying out to God for strength to rise above this persecution, I became angry with God and did what I knew best when I was afraid–I ran and hid, only this time I was hiding from my heavenly Father. My only understanding of what an earthly father was like was that I was a victim of his wrath. Many Christians today (or non-Christians) are driven away from a relationship with God because their unhealed pasts give them an unhealthy basis upon which to approach their Heavenly Father. I remember at 16 when I faced this persecution, I ran out into a hay field and laid on my face and sobbed for hours. I was sure that God had given up on me because I could not serve Him. I also believed a lie that God must not love me, and maybe He never really did love me-no one else had.

Looking back on my life, that was the day that many doors were opened to rejection, despair, depression, suicide and religion. (These are all spirits and I will speak more about this realization later). The depth of rejection and despair reached a low in me. Even tears could not seem to relieve the pain. I was a victim again.

From that point, I somehow rose up and turned my foster father in for abuse. I was accused of fabricating all my reports. No investigation was filed on the foster care home. In fact, they were preparing to send me to a reform school of sorts. I appealed to my biological mother who was willing and able to get custody of my sister and I. All these events could have caused deep roots of bitterness to set in, but God had other plans.

The odd fact about an abused person is that they have a distorted sense of acceptance and love. Words like trust are not "user-friendly" to a victim of abuse. As a child you tend to shift into a survival phase by living day to day with a vigilant attitude

31

but being very insecure and always asking, "what's next?"

I would like to move forward in time now, to when I was about 20 years old. The first abusive partner was someone I had simply "wound" up with. I didn't choose him, he chose me. He came to visit with a friend of mine from Kansas City and never left. I couldn't get him to leave. He was basically living in benefit of my social inadequacies. Odd as this might seem, I had let down my moral standards for my life. We lived as ships passing in the night (I know now was a sinful lifestyle) and somehow this became a strange "used" relationship of 11 years. We were married after ten years. Unfortunately love had very little to do with this decision. I felt like a victim the first day I met him and he began to use me. Spiritually, I was in a backslidden state. Although I knew Jesus, I had never been taught anything about how to live and I did not know that there was a Holy Spirit that could be resident in me to strengthen, comfort and guide me. I was carnal and very much on my own, or so I thought. I became pregnant by this man who was very verbally and physically abusive. One time at Christmas he had destroyed all of the gifts I had made and purchased for my family and blackened my right eye, cheek and then wrapped a chain around my neck and dragged me around the apartment. Eventually, he left me and went to

Kansas City. I was relieved. I thought maybe now I can actually start a new life with the baby.

When I was 8 months pregnant, I moved into a new apartment. Before I was completely moved in (many boxes were still sitting unpacked and some things were not moved in yet), there was a knock at my back door. I curiously opened the door a crack and suddenly, a stranger broke into the apartment with a knife in one hand and pornographic pictures in the other. The stack of pictures hit the floor as fast as I remember my body being thrown to the floor. Immediately, I felt the weight of this perpetrator who painfully slammed upon my pregnant belly. (He was very large and much stronger than I was and eventually I was beaten beyond recognition). Early on, I had gotten the knife away from him and hurled it into the ceiling so I would not have to worry about it. He became very angry when I fought. At one point, he was trying to throw me into the bathtub and he kicked me violently in the pregnant belly. From room to room I struggled to try to escape but he would catch me and beat me as if he was trying to knock me out. This struggle went on for one hour and I screamed for help throughout the hour but no one heard me. No one came. I know that I am alive today because I cried out to my Father God during this beating-the one I had turned my back on. People say that your life flashes before you with near death experiences and this is what happened to me. I saw the headlines in the newspaper- "Victim of a Brutal Attack Found". I cried out to God, "If you can hear me save me please! Save my baby! Please don't let us die." I was weak , and ready to pass out.

After an hour of beating by this perpetrator, he had me pinned by the neck to the kitchen wall and was choking me. I had tried to run out of the kitchen door but he had promptly put my body through the door and glass shattered all over me. I was lifeless against the wall-his face was so close that his breath was right in mine. I believe at that moment the Lord spoke to me and said, "Tell him that you forgive him for what he's done to you." At this point, I was totally blinded. The beating to my eyes and face had caused a "hydracephalic-type" swelling over my eye sockets and no light could get in to see. I felt-what have I got to lose? If God is really speaking to me, then I had better get my heart right for this plan to work. I said in a whisper to the man, "Look at me. Take a good look at what you have done to me." I was so weak, I was barely conscious due to the loss of blood. There was only his breath on my face and a panting sound. I said, "I want you to know that I forgive you for doing this to me." When I said those words, it was as if an angel came into the room. I began to see a brilliant white light (remember I had no sight in the natural). Suddenly, I felt as if something had lifted his weight off of me and it sounded like his body flew back on the floor. I still could not see anything.

I only heard noises and saw this brilliant white light. Now from a distance, across the room, I heard a voice say, "You can go". It took every bit of energy I could muster up along with shots of newfound adrenalin to move. I stood to my feet and followed the white light out of the building. I felt the walls with my hands and heard broken glass crunching under my bare feet as this glorious light led me down the stairs to the outside. I was in a state of shock. I continued to follow the light, as I still had no sight at all. God's strength carried each footstep, one in front of the other, as I was so weak. I found myself collapsing and felt strong arms grab me, which broke my fall. It was a volunteer fireman on his way to a fire. The light had brought me right into his path. He caught and carried me to his apartment where he called the ambulance and police for me. My baby girl was pronounced dead at the hospital later on that evening, due to a fractured skull. After this incident I remember someone saying, "How could a loving God allow this to happen".

For the first time in years I was able to say, "We don't always understand why we go through some things, but I know that it was God who delivered me out of the hands of that madman, and I had truly forgiven him–only by the grace of God."

I had clearly developed a victim mentality throughout my life, but isn't it strange that God used a tragic moment such as this where I was actually a victim to show me that He really had a plan for my life. God took what Satan meant to use to destroy me and created a turning point through which He could renew my life and draw me back to salvation, as my life was being destroyed without Him. I began to see that no matter what happens in my life, God has never left me. It was I who had left Him. I had lived under this victim mentality to a point of unhealthy thinking and despite the breakthrough that God had given me I still had a long way to go.

My husband came back into my life when the baby died and although he was a drunk and abusive, I thought of nothing else but to have a baby -someone I could really love and who would love me back. God was merciful to me and one year later a beautiful son was born to me. I felt that my life was being restored. God was drawing me and I had not yet found how dear God could be to me. I had never been able to draw close to God and find this love I lacked, this acceptance that I had desperately craved. Is it possible that God can love me that way? Where does such insecurity come from?

Please allow me to reflect on some characteristics of a victim mentality that are especially seen in an adult child of an alcoholic. Note that not all females or males in abusive situations possess these characteristics. In some cases, as indicated in "No Place to Cry"(Van Stone, D & Lutzer, E.W. 1990, Moody pp. 46-47), either directly or indirectly, the abused believe that because they were abused in their youth they deserve to continue to be abused as adults. Van Stone/Lutzner stated that there is an actual bonding to abuse that takes place, which causes the abused person to actively play the role of a victim. In a further description of "bonding to abuse", these individuals caught in a cycle of abuse may be more difficult ones to break free, simply because they play the role of the victim with no plans to "rise above the situation-devoid of all hope of a better life". In extreme cases, a passive victim may seek out an abusive partner, because this victim believes that they do not deserve to be treated well. They may in some cases even reject genuine love when it is offered and may self-sabotage any love offered making future rejection inevitable." Others play an aggressive role in the inflicting of torment. They look for people that they can harm convinced that their victims deserve to be abused. Very often, they deny being responsible in any way and blame the victim). Whether "actively or passively, abuse victims often may perpetuate the abuse." (Vanstone, Lutzner).

Social learning theorists believe that children who witness a parent being abused or who perhaps are victims themselves are higher risk for abuse as they have reportedly lower self-esteem. (Laird-McCue, M. "Domestic Violence",1995).

It is my personal experience, that children and women who live in domestic violence may show symptoms of Post-Traumatic Stress syndrome manifesting in nightmares, difficulty sleeping, eating disorders, attending problems, flashbacks, anxiety, etc. There are many more symptoms of abuse that have been noted that negatively affect children which I will discuss more in later chapters. It is not practical to think that we as a society can stop all children from being subjected to domestic violence, although it should be a major focus by all health professionals and social systems workers. However, I do believe that if we are going to impact our future generations in order to stop further situations of domestic violence, we need to speak positively into the lives of our children.

Through early intervention, we can educate children who are victims of domestic violence in order that we may stop the cycle of abuse. We may better be able to identify those who simply may be targets for abusers or to identify weak areas in their young characters early.

Educators can proactively feed children positive information about how:

1. They can break the cycle of abuse.

2. To identify unacceptable ways to be treated.
3. To set boundaries to protect themselves.

4. They can set their own healthy thinking patterns, despite what is happening around them.

5. To make a stand and learn to "rise above" a victim mentality.

Children need to be accepted, loved, and they need someone to talk to that they can trust. Often children in these situations do not find these kinds of supports as readily as they need to. I do wish that someone had spoken to me at an <u>early</u> age about how valuable I am to God. He has created me with a destiny on my life and that despite everything, God always has had a plan for my life. He sent His son Jesus to be the victim so that I could be victorious. I do not need to be the victim ever again. Please take a moment to pray this prayer with me:

Dear Father in Heaven, thank you that you are forgiving me of all sin.

Thank you for the strength that only you can give to me.

Thank you that you are drawing me by your word.

Thank you for safety and security.

Thank you for loving me and for giving me a clear vision that you do have a plan for my life even if I don't understand what that plan is yet.

Thank you for leading and guiding me in all my decisions. Forgive me of all sin.

Thank you that you are renewing my mind

Come into my heart and be Lord of my life. Please help me to surrender the 'victim mindset' to you so that I can be victorious.

I take back any authority I may have given to the devil through this victim mentality and I give that authority back to my Lord Jesus Christ.

I choose to break the yoke of that victim mentality in the name of Jesus.

I choose to bind the victim mentality in the name of Jesus and I ask Lord that you fill me to overflowing with your Holy Spirit.

> *In Jesus name. Amen*

CHAPTER 4

YET ANOTHER FIRE

At this point, I will be describing some events that took place after I had begun a new Christian life with my son. I was involved with a church that worked to counsel the situation but my ex-husband chose to leave us both without contest and we were divorced within a year. Though it was not God's best choice, it is scriptural that if the unbelieving mate chooses to leave then the other mate can be given a release from this situation of abandonment-or so I was told at the time. I was still in need of teaching but after the divorce I began to grow by leaps and bounds.

I was being restored. God called me back to Him when my son was just a newborn. God spoke to me audibly one day while I was alone in the living room. He said, "Go get your bible". I seriously began to tremble. I had not read the bible in 12 years. The trembling continued as I searched through a dusty box to dig out the only bible that I knew was in my apartment. It was an old friend's bible that was left with a few of her things that she had never picked up. Silly as all of this may sound, I ran to the living room where I had heard the voice and I asked, "What do you want, Lord?" God told me to read Daniel 3:1-30. This was the story of Shadrach, Meshach, and Abed-nego. These three young men were thrown into a fiery furnace for not bowing down to the idol that King Nebuchadnezzar had commanded them to worship. God delivered them safely out of the fire without so much as a hair singed on their heads. Witnesses had said that those who had the misfortune of throwing the men into the furnace were killed from the intensity of the heat. While the three men were in the fire others saw the image of a fourth man. It was the image of the Son of God who was with them. After reading this amazing story, suddenly a gospel group on the T.V. began to sing the story of Shadrach, Meshach, and Abed-nego. This was too weird. I then became obsessed with reading God's word. It was something I now had to do on a daily basis.

Then God called me to go to church. I am not trying to sound spooky-spiritual. I knew God was telling me to go to church but I did not know where to go. I would get up on Sunday mornings and dress my son and myself but then I would not go anywhere. Finally, one day I did a random point in the yellow pages and I went to the Free Methodist Church. I walked in that Sunday and guess what the sermon was about? You guessed it-Shadrach, Meshach, and Abed-nego!

I rededicated my life to the Lord that Sunday and continued to listen for God's voice daily. He told me to go to a Pentecostal Church where I received the baptism of the Holy Spirit. When I remember that day I am flooded with the everlasting love that God has for me. Though I knew nothing about the Holy Spirit, God baptized me with the Holy Spirit with the evidence of speaking in tongues (WITH FIRE!). What on earth is that you say? My thoughts exactly! I stood next to an eleven-year old boy and with arms lifted high to God we both spoke in a heavenly language before God (1 Corinthians 12). Was this for real? Was this natural? This was a supernatural experience-one like I had never known before. I remember my natural mind saying, "You fool-what on earth do you think you are doing?" I also had a sensation of power surging through both arms as something coming from heaven. It surged through me and consumed every part of my being. From what I understand, not every person who asks God for the baptism of the Holy Spirit has this same experience, so I guess it's a FAITH thing. If you do ask the Lord for the baptism of the Holy Spirit, believe that you have received it. Whether you have any feelings or not, know that you have received!

We are all spiritual beings created in the image of God. I have always found it interesting that so many movies, books and millions of dollars are spent on psychic phenomenon. People are so eager to hear about "demons", "hauntings" or soothsaying words from an icy grave, yet you mention the power of the Holy Spirit and people think you've lost your faculties. In reality, people are starved for the supernatural-they yearn for spiritual things to satisfy the spiritual longing that was placed inside of them by God to begin with.

We receive God's promises by faith. For example, when we are saved, we are saved by faith. When we are asking God for the baptism of the Holy Spirit, we ask it of God in faith. God's word says, "Or what man is there of you, whom if his son asks for bread, will he give him a stone? Or if he asks of him a fish, will he give him a serpent? If ye then, being evil, know how to give good gifts unto your children, how much more shall your Father which is in heaven give good things to them that ask Him?"(Matthew7: 9) God has sent us His Holy Spirit so that we can be comforted in our walk of faith. He also tells us in the word that "the steps of a good man are ordered of the Lord, and he delights in his way." (Psalm 37:23) Further, God tells us, "A man's heart devises his way; but the Lord directs his steps." (Proverbs 16:9) The reason I am belaboring this is to bring a point home–that point is that God mercifully gave us the Holy Spirit to strengthen us to walk in the steps that He directs us to walk in and we walk by faith through the light of God's word. I may never have gotten quite as lost in the wasted years of domestic violence if I had known of the help of God's Holy Spirit at a much younger age. I was saved by faith, but almost perished time and time again because I lacked the strength, comfort and guidance that the Holy Spirit is able to provide for us through our walk of faith.

In addition, there was another destructive measure that I had operating in my life that I almost let get the best of me. I had opened many doors in my life to the wrong spiritual powers. Please allow me to explain. Earlier, I had disclosed the years of abuse that I had been exposed to and the despair that I had allowed to take hold of me when I was persecuted at 16 years of age. This manifested in rejection, depression, spirit of suicide, fear, religion, and lust. Unfair as it may seem, these spirits can invade a person through sexual abuse or fornication and unless we cleanse ourselves, these cause more problems. I also had opened up doors to the occult when I was in a backslidden state.

While longing for "spiritual things" I became involved with ouija boards, séances, talking to dead people, fortune telling, tarot cards, etc. I had no idea what kinds of spiritual problems I had acquired over the years. Sure I was saved, but I had not taken the steps to "renounce" and repent of opening these doors to the wrong kind of spiritual powers. It is amazing how many people do not believe that there is a devil or demonic powers. We may come to believe that Jesus Christ conquered the works of the devil but where we fall short is that we are slow to learn to walk out our faith against the darts or temptations that the devil continues to throw at us. Ephesians 6:10-18 tells us clearly,

"Finally, my brethren, be strong in the Lord, and in the power of His might. Put on the whole armour of God, that ye may be able to stand against the wiles of the devil." This bit of information–other than the good news of salvation–is the most important thing you will ever need to learn.

Why is this so related to my experiences of domestic violence? I had broken free of the cycle of abuse from my first marriage and was rededicated to God, filled with the Holy Spirit, and debt free, I thought nothing bad could ever happen to me. Still I fell into yet another "Fire"-WHY? - Because there were **spiritual doors** still open that could only be closed by renouncing the activities or sins that I had committed that opened the doors to begin with. With the authority of Jesus Christ, I needed to break the yokes of those spirits of abuse, rage, violence, bind and rebuke (or stop) those spirits from influencing my life any further. In addition, I needed to command the spirits to leave me and to ask God for a fresh filling of the Holy Spirit. All in Jesus name. Needless to say, I did not do this before I met my second husband and I was an easy target for this spirit of violence to prey on me. I was deceived into thinking that he was a man of God who was studying to be a minister and I was taken in by this deception. Now, you have a description of what can happen to spiritually draw a perpetrator to his victim. In later chapters, I will discuss the characteristics that are exhibited by those who are abusive. These characteristics are found to be common with all those who are abusive. If women are aware of these characteristics, it will enable them to be on guard for future relationships.

In simple children's words, every good gift is from above (God) and every bad thing is from below (Satan). Once a woman has fallen into domestic violence situation, and if she is not **delivered** (which means to repent, renounce, break the yoke, bind the spirits, all in the name of Jesus, and be filled up with the Holy Spirit) then she is easy prey for another abusive perpetrator. Deliverance or no deliverance, it is wise to wait two to three years before entering into another relationship to allow healing to happen within. Though we can explain things in terms of "characteristics" when we talk about the abusive person, remember, these characteristics are all driven by evil spiritual entities. Always keep that in mind when dealing with any power of darkness that it is out to kill, steal and destroy. Always put on your spiritual armour everyday. Use the name of Jesus when renouncing and learn to take back any authority that you gave to the devil. Give that authority back to the Lord Jesus Christ on a daily basis as you meet with challenges. If you can get help with your prayers for deliverance from a pastor or elder of a church, that would be the best way to go.

I hope that this chapter has opened up your eyes to the world of the "spiritual". More importantly, know that God sent us His Holy Spirit to help us learn more of what is true, to assist us in our walk of faith and with our battles against the devil. My pastor did an excellent teaching on intercessory prayer, which gave an example of what happens in the spirit realm when doors are left open. He said, "It is so important to ensure that you close doors that had been opened through sin in our lives –either through repentance or in some cases through renouncing any authority you gave to the devil. Give that authority back to our Lord Jesus Christ and then ask the Holy Spirit to come and fill you up (as mentioned earlier). Pastor also went on to say that as you do spiritual warfare, (which is praying earnestly for others) if some areas in your life are still open to powers that have been given to the devil, and are in need of healing, it's like having open, bleeding wounds and swimming in a "spiritual" shark tank (the shark being the powers of the devil). The rest is history. 1Corinthians 10:4 says, "For the weapons of our warfare are not carnal, but mighty in God for pulling down strongholds, casting down imaginations, and every high thing that exalts itself against the knowledge of God, and bringing into captivity every thought to the obedience of Christ."

We need to know that we have the victory through Christ but that there is a raging spiritual battle for your salvation, for your faith. The devil loves it when people don't wise up to his tactics. Know that any kind of bondage starts in the spiritual and manifests in the natural. We need to stay spiritually alert and at war against the devil in order to have the strength to overcome abuse in our lives and in our children's lives as well.

Joyce Meyers once said comically during a sermon, "You know, so many people struggle with who they are and many do not know. Many don't have a clue where they are going when they die, but they seem to be in an awful hurry to get there." This is sadly quite true. There are so many mystifying spiritual intrigues in this day and age and unfortunately, people who are hungry for spiritual things are so often deceived. We are all created by God to be spiritual beings, made in the image of God the Father, Jesus and the Holy Spirit. Let's face it-if we don't know that Jesus is the Son of the only true God in every thing that we do, then we may find ourselves worshipping and giving over power in our lives to false gods, or other idols and spiritual intrigues. Though we may think it most innocent, doors are opened to demonic powers and we need to close them. As a part of the battle, it is an ongoing process for those who have been wounded by domestic violence, to continue to take back authority and not to let the devil lie to you about who you are. God loves you and you are His righteousness.

Please take a moment to pray this prayer with me.

Jesus, thank You for forgiving me of all sin.

Thank you for dying on the cross for me so that I may be saved and have the power through Your Holy Spirit to make the right decisions, and to be filled with strength.

Please come in to this body and fill me with your Holy Spirit.

I want to receive your baptism with fire and a heavenly language to speak to you with.

Please teach me your truths and help me to walk in the walk of faith.

Help me to make a decision to change my life Lord.

I surrender all that I am to You.

Please help me to learn how to take authority in my home, my life and place a spiritual, physical, mental, emotional, moral, and financial hedge of protection over me and all my children and family members.

> *in Jesus Name, Amen.*

CHAPTER 5
BROKEN COVENANTS

I have spent a lot of time sharing my own life experiences because I felt for years while I lived in the domestic violence that no one could ever know my pain. I thought no one could understand how difficult it was to stand in faith that my life could change. I believed this lie primarily because I was kept isolated from other Christians. I have taken great time in these writings to lay some principle foundation of how lovingly God drew me out and planted my feet in a place where they would not slip away. In spite of what I lived through, the one truth that was brought home to me was, had I not returned to God, and looked to Him for strength, I would not be alive today.

Unfortunately, there are some women that do **not** live as a result of the abuse that they endured. Each year, thousands of American women are killed by their husbands or intimate partners. It is so important to understand that when we think that no one knows, God <u>**always**</u> knows exactly where we are and He patiently waits for fruit to be seen in His children's' lives.

One evening, the Lord awakened me at about 3 a.m. He said to me, "Where is thy fruit?" He repeated this several times and all I could do was weep.

It is important to examine the fruit that we see from our lives as well as the fruit coming from the lives of those we are sharing a relationship with. What do I mean by this? In order to have healthy relationships, it is imperative that we compliment and enhance each other in the things that we do. This was an area that was so evident with my second husband. He was supposed to be a man of God yet there was no good fruit.

Please clearly note that **abuse** is unacceptable no matter what your faith or belief system is. It is a **criminal act**. Husbands have no right treating their wives and children in an abusive manner. (I believe that battering is violence against the whole family-not just against the wife.)

The bible tells us how to treat each other. Matthew 7:12 states, "Therefore, whatsoever ye would that men should do to you, do ye even so to them." Matthew 7:16 states, "Ye shall know them by their fruits. Do men gather grapes of thorns or figs of thistles? Even so every good tree brings forth good fruit, but a corrupt tree brings forth evil fruit." This was what I saw for the last 12 years of our marriage. The man that I married was supposed to be a minister, yet all the fruit that was apparent on a daily basis was evil. This created a great contradiction within me. I was living a lie yet I was "praying" for God to make a divine breakthrough in our lives.

The following excerpts are from Dave Wilkerson's Times Square Church pulpit series newsletter entitled, "The Measured Glory of God"10/00. "Until we all come in the unity of the faith unto the measure of the stature of the fullness of Christ" Ephesians 4:13. The apostle Paul is saying two things:

1. If we're going to live God's way-sober-minded and with intensity, our goal should be to have an ever-increasing measure of His glory, until we enter into full maturity in Christ.

2. The measure of faith we have all been given is meant to **serve and supply the rest of the body of Christ.** This of course includes all husbands, wives, widows etc.

Ephesians 4:16"says, "According to the effectual working in the measure of every part, (making) increase of the body unto the edifying of itself in love." Now Paul is talking about the church as a whole, despite what denomination any of us are.

In history, specifically in 1874, it was recorded in the laws that a man could beat his wife providing that the tool he used to beat her was no larger in diameter than the size of his thumb, hence-the expression rule of thumb. It was expected that he did not break any bones and in general it was the "man's business to keep his woman in line."

Although by the grace of God this legislature was overthrown, we as women have still lived under a shadow of this societal belief, which was a standard in every church, synagogue etc. Unfortunately this attitude still lingers in today's churches (i.e. "what's going on is their business. It's not up to us to meddle"). In some cases, the churches simply do not know what approach to take or what to do about women and children in a domestic violence situation. Many believe that married couples have entered into a covenant relationship and it is a sacred place that women should stand by her man and pray that the marriage is healed. It is my conviction that when the husband chooses to abuse his family and puts any one of their lives in danger, then he has **already broken the covenant** that he made as a husband pledging his life to his wife.

In my case, I believed God was going to enhance my situation. I can say this now, "Yes, God can do anything, but women and children should **not tolerate** abuse for any reason and should not stay in this environment. GET OUT and believe God somewhere else, where it is safe.

Let's get back to what the apostle Paul was saying about serving and supplying the rest of the body. We as a church (to include all denominations) need to unite to serve and supply the rest of the body with a plan of action, system of supports, and education and training with regard to the intense needs of a member in an abusive situation.

Paul is also saying that every one of us is a working member of the body of Christ (the church)- a joint here a muscle there. We, being such life-giving entities, are to supply an ever-increasing measure of health to the other members of the church. We are each designed to be a source of faith, love, mercy, grace, and glory working together to produce a stronger, healthier body (church). (Wilkerson,10/00)

The health of the church as a body of course depends on each of us being in good health. If one of us is blessed, the whole church is blessed. Likewise, if one church member sins, then the whole body is affected. Mr. Wilkerson asks the question, "How much health, that is how much glory and faith, are you supplying to Christ's body of believers" (or to His church)? Is God's love increasing in you daily? Also, are you able to supply strength to other body members? To all these questions, when I was immersed in the abusive lifestyle, I had to answer "**no, no, and no**". I was not increasing in God's love daily. I was not supplying strength to other members. God's glory and faith, though it was resident in me, was not freely flowing to other members of the church. I do not want you to get into condemnation, nor am I condemning myself. If you have been there and you haven't been able to get your plan in motion to get out, know that **God still loves you**. (I'm just trying to spell out what I saw come together that finally put an end to the abuse we were living in.)

Most obviously, my situation did not strengthen the body and a church needs to know that a solid plan of action for victims of domestic violence needs to be a part of protocol. A woman in this kind of situation learns to survive because that's all they know to do in order to stay alive and to keep the children alive. (Many dedicated and trained supports and advocates need to be lined up to work with the woman to develop a plan of action, to rehearse that plan, and to provide shelter for the woman and children.)

Abused women also need supports that will work with her to provide a plan to keep them all away from this perpetrator. These supports need to be in place for an indefinite period of time. The perpetrator's goal in life is to force reconciliation so that the woman winds up back at his battering post. He will stop at nothing, i.e. especially court hearings to work on the civil court system to try and manipulate the situation in order to gain unsupervised visitation and power over his victims once again. Batterers in court often pretend to be the caring fathers for a strategic purpose to gain access to the women and children.

In general, if fruit is not seen in our lives as believers in Christ, it is as if Christ has laid down His life in vain. It is a break in the covenant with our Father who has provided all the supernatural supports we need .We, in turn, need to do the work to reach out to our church members to repair the breaks in the walls of the house of God. I am so thankful that a group of members from my church stepped forward to support my daughter and I through court mandated supervised visitation. If this support was not there for me, I may not have gotten the support in criminal court that I did the last time I tried to break free.

In later chapters I will go into more detail about the characteristics of an abusive or unsafe husband or mate. I will also discuss about the civil court, criminal court and Supreme Court orders of protection. Every woman in a domestic violence situation should have at least one, if not all 3, types of court orders.

Please take a minute to pray this prayer with me:

Dear Father, thank You for loving me and for forgiving me of all my sins.

Thank You for being Lord of my life, for filling me with your Holy Spirit and providing all the supernatural supports that I need.

Please send me a plan and a sound direction that I may go in.

Direct my steps and cause me to truly know that I can fight the good fight of faith with your help.

Help me to stand firm for what is right and true and let my life bear much fruit for You my Lord.

In Jesus Name I pray, Amen.

Psalm 1:1-3

"Blessed is the man that walks not in the counsel of the ungodly, nor stands in the way of sinners, nor sits in the seat of the scornful, but his delight is in the law of the Lord, and in His law doth he meditate day and night. And he shall be like a tree planted by the rivers of water, that brings forth his **fruit** in his season; his leaf also shall not wither, and whatsoever he does shall prosper."

CHAPTER 6

BREAKTHROUGH

One day several years ago, something rose up inside of me. It was faith. Suddenly, I knew my God was alive. Oh, He had spoken to me; saved my life countless times, but all at once I knew that He was going to deliver us out of the pit of violence we were in. I knew that I knew.

My three children and I were being victimized by my second husband who was drunk and quite out of control. At the time, my oldest son was ten years, my middle son was four years, and my daughter was two years old. My husband began screaming uncontrollably- that was our cue to run for cover. We found ourselves in the nearest bedroom, which was a far drop to the ground as we lived in a split-level ranch. It appeared as if we were quite trapped. I remember speaking the name of Jesus over the situation. I professed that Jesus was Lord over what was happening, despite what we saw. We could hear glass breaking and horrible crashing sounds. My oldest son was on the top bunk bed and I sat on the floor with the two little ones. I began to sing praises to my Lord, and as I sang the children began to sing with me despite their fear and distraction. Every so often, we would hear large destructive sounds as if everything in the house was being destroyed. We later saw that everything had been destroyed. He had thrown a Television through a plate glass window and the house had a hole in the wall.

My husband would periodically come up to the bedroom door and pound it to instill terror and intimidation. He would yell in to us, "I'm going to kill you all one at a time." Then we would hear another crash. We continued to lift up praises to the Lord even in the midst of this horrible situation.

After praising the Lord, I felt God gave me the strength to get us out of there. I sensed an assurance that we would not be harmed in any way. This was a breakthrough in thinking as I was so immobilized with fear that usually I would do nothing.

I first lowered my oldest son out of the window on a bed sheet I then lowered the 2 smaller children out to him and told them to be very quiet. I then jumped to the ground with my car keys (which I often kept with me-again survival). And we ran to the car. I got the kids in the car and I was just about to open the driver's door when the front door of the house tore open-a maniac was running straight at me. He grabbed me by the throat and began to strangle me. Before he could apply pressure, I remembered the assurance that I had received from God-we would not be hurt. I said to my husband "In the name of Jesus get your hands off of me!" He let go of me; I backed away, got in the car and drove away with the children. I called the police (another breakthrough) and pressed charges at this time he was already facing up to 25 years in prison. We were separated for about 2 years. This was the beginning of what would be a very **long** end.

As I had described in Chapter 1, you have to make a decision to get out. I had made a decision that we were not going to live in a state of fear and immobility anymore. My life began to change at this point. My husband had gone to a Christian rehabilitation facility in Chicago for six months, which served him well in releasing him from prison time.

I remained separated from him after he came out of rehabilitation. He had revisited court to get the order of protection altered to the point that he could see his children without supervision and we were basically at a forced reconciliation point. Many women today face these court proceedings and without much support and advocacy the civil court hassle often breaks her down.

I will soon get to my final freedom breakthrough, but I would like to make a point right now. The process that protected me from a forced reconciliation the last time we went through court proceedings was that I had both a civil court and a criminal court order of protection against my husband. Most women in domestic violence situations do not know that they have a right to civil, criminal, and supreme court orders of protection (supreme can be obtained if she is pursuing a divorce). Please listen to this: In every case of domestic violence, the man can be charged with a criminal activity-no matter how small. When criminal charges are filed, then the arresting and investigating officers can temporarily issue a criminal order. There have been occasions that a woman has been denied this criminal order of protection if she neglects to get the officer to deal with it before he leaves the investigation. I also know how much courage it takes to file charges, and to write statements against your abuser. The temptation is great to minimize what damage has been done. It is likely that when an incident happens, and the police are involved, the women who are being abused are often afraid to press charges. Further, if they do press charges, the abuser presses with threats to get them to drop the charges. In my case, I pressed charges against my abuser and he was bailed out the very next day.

You face the reality that he may want to come back to punish you. I experienced this time and time again. This struggle is the one I referred to in Chapter 1– you have to be ready to make a plan and stick with it to remain safe. Once you have been granted an order of protection, charges *must* be pressed against your abusers when they fail to follow what the order of protection says. This also takes a lot of courage. Is the consistency worth it? Yes! Is it hard to do? Again, **Yes**! You need to keep your focus because your freedom is worth it.

You will need to use the court system for help, so become aware of how to educate the courts of your situation. Here is an example of why this can be helpful: My husband could not override in civil court what the criminal court had established-thank you, God! Also, my husband could not break down the visitation demands for mandated supervision, which is easy to do in civil court, because the criminal court order held firm–no contact. The abuser uses the children and visitation to further put the abusive squeeze on the family in order to force reconciliation. Most people on the outside find it difficult to know what to do to help the women and children and often stand in amazement that the women ends up with the abuser again. What family advocates and even family court need to know is that standards of visitation need to be reevaluated when it comes to cases where there has clearly been a history of abuse. I believe that a domestic violence assessment should be mandated of the accused abuser. Where there is a determined finding of a history of violence, then all visitation rights should be suspended until proof of counsel for abusive characteristics can be demonstrated to the civil court by the alleged abuser.

I had first hand experience with the idiom "a man deserves his day in court". Our abuser had rallied around a new method of abusing all of us and that was by repeatedly dragging us back to court. There were times one summer that we were literally in court every week. Now having said all of that–where was I? Oh yes, I had decided that we were going to be free of this tyranny.

In respect of my new level of faith, I began to sing for the church choir. It was something I had lost my nerve, or desire to do. I had a gift to sing and before I was married this last time I used to travel all over New York and sing for God and bring people to the saving knowledge of Christ. I had been in the church for six years and I had not been obedient to sing for God. As I explained earlier, my fruit was not seen.

I began to seek the Lord through worship, prayer and reading the bible and I began resisting the devil through intercession (which is earnestly seeking God on behalf of others).

I decided that my life was going to show some fruit. I wanted to share the love of Christ with others. Though I was greatly rejected by most people, I continued to press in to the things of the Lord. I so wanted fruit to be seen. The greatest fruit God was drawing me to produce was to bring others who were lonely and emotionally devastated to salvation and to let them know that all things are possible. How does all this come together? From the point in time I described early on in this chapter to the present, every destructive act that our abuser committed was reported. Of course he was not taken in on most of these acts, but I recognized it as unacceptable. To attempt to summarize some of this saga, he abstained from alcohol for four years. This did not stop his abusive qualities; it just kept his abuse more to the level of emotional, spiritual and verbal.

Incidentally, it is a myth that alcohol causes abuse. This myth is even believed by many people still entangled in domestic violence. An abuser is an abuser! It is a proven statistic that it is not the alcohol that induces the abuse-it is usually just a good excuse. Often, abusers are mandated to go to treatment centers for alcohol and drug use and little is done to provide them treatment for abusive characteristics.

After the four-year reprieve from violent destructive acts, our abuser began to drink and use drugs again. When he became drunk he would have affairs and smash objects. In my years with him we had about seven telephones destroyed (that was the first thing to go), six table and chair sets, two television sets, several antiques, cupboards, toys, vases, countless dish sets, glasses, and many favorite possessions. He knew that I spent a fortune rebuilding the action on an antique oak piano with ornate carvings from the Victorian period. He wanted to hurt me so that during one episode he took an ax to the handcarved part and scraped the beautiful markings off. He then shot holes in the keyboard to be sure it was rendered useless.

I would go to church faithfully and I continued to be on the worship team. I also continued to press charges for these actions, which he would usually get out of. My abuser's family was always bailing him out of jail. Sometimes, it seems to me that families think they are helping the abuser by doing this. Perhaps it's a form of denial that the loved one has a problem. There was a case recently in the newspaper where the father bailed the abuser out of jail. Two days later, his estranged wife had made arrangements with the abuser's mother to pick up an important document (she did have an order of protection against him).

When she stopped by briefly after work to pick up the paper, the abuser met her in the garage of his parent's house and shot her. He then shot himself –leaving three children without parents. The abuser's mother was right in the kitchen, which was next to the garage.

Many of the violent actions displayed by my abuser were meant to put me in the state of immobility and force me to do what he wanted me to do. I no longer would buy into this game and this made his behavior even worse. The abusive person wants to control his victim. I had made up my mind that this tyranny was going to end, but I also felt strongly that it had to be in the Lord's timing or we may not have survived. The more I grew in the Lord, the more violent he became.

I worked on and completed my master's degree in the midst of a lot of dysfunction. Through all of this, God was teaching me, strengthening me, healing me and getting me ready for the day of BREAKTHROUGH! I have had so many people look at me as being evil for staying in this situation, but I know the fruit of Christ was unfolding in me. I cried out for God to break through in our lives. God, this has to stop!

The breakthrough finally came when the last episode of destruction our abuser had caused totaled $5835.00 worth of damage on our new home. He was discharging a high-powered rifle into his truck engine through the sliding glass doors of the house. My daughter and I were participating in a 21-day fast with the church. It was January 13th. We had not even completed the fast yet, but God was already in the process of our breakthrough. The children did not come home on the bus, as a part of our regular survival plans. They routinely did not stay alone with the abuser.

This particular day, all after school activities had been cancelled due to weather predictions and the children came home on the bus. Unfortunately, they had to witness yet another display of destruction. Most thankfully, it would be the very last. This time was our time to be free! When I filed for my civil court order of protection, and revisited court, I was granted a two-year civil court order of protection. My domestic violence advocate told me that she had never seen that happen in civil court. I had obtained a criminal court order of protection the day of the incident. Then later, when we revisited court, I was granted a five-year criminal order of protection. Again, this was God! Now many other orders in the past were obtained but my abuser would barrage me in court until he would break the orders down to the point that allowed him no restrictions and he could legally come near us. As I had described earlier, our abuser tried to barrage again in court. Only this time was the timing of God. Everything lined up-including supports from the church. There was a time period where we were fighting in court when the court mandated supervised visitations. We had revisited the court over five different times about the same issue. There were many women that were willing, and I might say very courageous, to assist me through this time. It had been mandated by the court to provide supervised visitation one time weekly for my daughter and her father. These supportive women were pioneers! They would tell him that he had to keep the conversations focused on healthy topics and to stay away from meddling or controlling issues that would put more pressure on my daughter. He did not like this and at one point he said to one of the women, "You can't tell me how to talk to my daughter," The brave pioneer answered, "Then this visit is over."

I could not have gotten through this difficult time had it not been for these women providing wonderful supports. They also made it easier for my daughter to get through this time.

Our abuser is now serving time in prison. When he was sentenced for this activity, he became enraged and attacked the deputy who escorted him to these proceedings at Grand Jury. The ambulance took the deputy away. It was said that he might have broken the deputy's arm.

During the 16 years of our marriage, there was no fruit of love, faith, mercy, grace or glory given to God or others that were impacted by the relationship. Many people were being destroyed.

Sometimes, even though I don't believe that God puts things like an abusive relationship on us; we have to know that He is a God of His word. Romans 8:28 says, "And we know that all things work together for good to them that love God, to them who are the called according to His purpose." So God will always take what the devil has meant to destroy us with and He will turn it around and make good come out of that situation because of how much He loves us.

Please take a moment to say this prayer with me:

Thank you Lord that you have worked everything together in my life for good to come out of my life.

I choose to surrender those things in my life that I have not given to you already, dear God.

I know that You have saved me, set me free, and filled me with Your precious Holy Spirit.

Thank You Lord. Now I beseech you, Lord, make my life one that shows forth good fruit for Your glory and according to Your purpose in me.

Thank You that You are the God of breakthrough. Thank You that no matter what I see with my eyes, You have provided me a breakthrough in this situation in my life.

My thoughts and my belief systems are changing. Help me to know that in You, I can do all things.

In Jesus name, Amen.

CHAPTER 7
WILL THESE DRY BONES LIVE?

God sometimes has us walk in dry, deserted places to bring us to our knees and to a place of complete dependence on Him. Please know that God is not putting any of the negative things on us that we go through just to teach us a lesson-God is not like that.

I have shared in nursing homes for about 25 years and here is a scripture that God has given me repeatedly throughout the years to share with those who may be feeling that they are totally alone. Isaiah 44:2 " Thus saith the Lord that made thee, and formed thee from the womb, which will help thee; fear not, O Jacob (Interject your name here), my servant; and thou Jerusalem, whom I have chosen." We are all precious in God's eyes and as long as we have the breath of life in us God has a destiny for each of us. When we know Jesus that is an eternal promise.

As I have pointed out in Chapter 6, God will use every situation in our lives to create good if we can learn to trust in Him. We do, however, desperately need His breath of life to revive us and our families back to a place filled with life-just like the dry bones in Ezekiel. A lifestyle for years of being on the vigil, of having been constantly put down, of having plan A, B, C, and D just to get through every waking day safely can wear you and your children down. You may be at a point where you discover that you have not really been alive nor do you feel alive now even though you are finally "free" to **really be** alive.

Living years in a state of abuse can leave you feeling like Ezekiel 37:3-4. The Lord said to Ezekiel in verse 3, " 'Son of man can these bones live?' And I answered Oh Lord God, 'You Know.' Again, He said unto me, 'Prophesy upon these bones, and say unto them, "Oh ye dry bones, hear the word of the Lord." I love this scripture. It was actually talking about re-establishing hope for the restoration of the nation Israel.

After a woman and her children have survived a domestic violence situation and all of the resulting fallout she may feel like "dry bones" She might even ask herself, "Can these bones live?" I remind you of what Ezekiel says back in verse 3: "Oh Lord God, You know."

God is the only one who carried you through all of the nightmare evenings, the moment of near death experience and the many lonely hours of loss that you simply were not able to share with your partner. You may experience remorse about not having a relationship that could have been something beautiful instead of what it really was. There will be times that you actually experience a feeling of loss and you may grieve almost as if you have lost a loved one through a death. You experience many free-floating emotions that you did not ever allow to surface while you lived day to day in survival mode.

This is all very normal and it is a good idea to find a good counselor who can help you work through some of these emotions that you were never able to truly show. After all, you learned that if you deny what is happening, then your abuser is much less combative and confrontive with you; so day in and day out you have learned to stuff your emotions. Some of these emotions that surface may include: insecurity, confusion, feelings of rejection, anger, hate, doubt, guilt, depression, unbelief, despair, loneliness, loss of control, bitterness and a feeling of anxiety almost as if you are more equipped for the bad news than the good. This, too, is normal but as the Lord said to Ezekiel "Prophesy upon these bones and say unto them, 'Oh ye dry bones, hear the word of the Lord.'"

If you have been with me up to this point, your newfound faith is ready to be worked. Unfortunately, I wish I could say that it was just going to happen, but the truth is you will need to "Speak to your dry bones". Tell yourself and your children, "This is a new beginning a new day. We are going to heal and resist all of those negative emotions." I am not saying you cannot feel as when you were in the pit of abuse, but, do not allow yourself to be overtaken and ruled by your emotions. Do not be overcome by evil, but overcome evil with good.

Prophesy life into your family, into those dry bones, know and have faith that you are on the road to recovery. Forgive those who have hurt you, daily seek God's help and know that it is not a sin to be tempted. Temptation will come, but we are not to be ruled by these emotions. It is a sin to listen and obey that temptation, the voice that calls you back to bondage. Galatians 5:1 says "Stand fast therefore in the liberty where with Christ hath made us free, and be not entangled again with the yoke of bondage." It is vitally important during this road to recovery to keep strong advocates, and positive supporters. This may mean you need to choose who you want to spend time with. Also, watch your confessions or the words that come out of your mouth. While the abundance of your heart is being renewed we need to bite our tongues. Speak blessings over yourself and your family.

When God says, "Prophesy to the bones", you can read the word of God daily to your children and to yourself, which brings life into all that you are, and into all that you do. Make a conscious effort to stay free. Establish in your mind (heart) first that you are "free at last". Allow God to repair and restore you. You may want to have a pastor pray with you. If you slip it is important to repent. Repeat the prayer we are going to pray below, and don't let the devil lie to you. He will surely try.

Please take a moment to say this prayer with me:

Thank you for salvation, forgiveness of sins, and the gift of the Holy Spirit.

Thank You, Lord, for freedom.

Now I choose to take back every bit of authority that I have given to the devil through fear, unbelief, rejection, hopelessness, doubt, (you name it), and I give all authority back to my Lord Jesus Christ.

Put your hand on your heart if you don't have a pastor or someone with faith to pray and say:

I break every yoke of demonic oppression that would bring fear, doubt, unbelief, hopelessness or rejection, in the name of Jesus. Now I bind all spirits of fear, unbelief, rejection, doubt, and hopelessness, in the name of Jesus.

The Lord God doth rebuke all these entities from this vessel and all these named bondages must leave me now in the name of Jesus.

Holy Spirit come, fill me to overflowing with Your power, fill up every space, I close every door to these things in the spirit.

In Jesus precious name, Amen.

Praise You, Lord.

CHAPTER 8
HOW DOES THIS CONCERN ME?

Are you being abused? For the most part, you have heard me tell my story and a personal account of how I was slowly drawn to freedom. The fact is, had I not made the decision to be free as indicated earlier, perhaps I would still be in bondage. I have read hundreds of accounts of women who are now free. One woman in particular made her decision and it took her five years to execute her plan of escape. For another, it took eight years, another ten years and as I shared earlier it took me twelve years. The point I want to make is that the earlier you are able to get away from the tyranny, the better!

You may want to ask yourself, "How does all of this concern me?" Am I in an abusive relationship? Some women do not even know the answer to this question.

There are some very useful abuse inventory checklists throughout the many resources listed in the back of this book. The very best abuse checklist I have discovered is from *7 Steps To Free Yourself From An Abusive Relationship* by Andrea Lissette. Andrea Lisette's inventory checklists may assist you in being able to define exactly where you are.

The first inventory checklist is one for **emotional abuse**. Lissette says that emotional abuse is usually the first type of abuse introduced in a relationship, which may precede other forms of abuse. It's simply a fact that if your partner is made aware that certain behaviors he exhibits cause you to feel abused and he continues to behave in that fashion, that would clearly be considered abuse. Does your partner...

- Accuse you of things you have not done?
- Act Jealous?
- Consistently ignore your feelings?
- Continually blame you for abusive incidents?
- Continually threaten to leave or divorce you?
- Criticize your race, culture, or gender?
- Degrade or humiliate you, your friends or your family?
- Deny you the right of your own opinion?
- Embarrass or disgrace you?
- Insist that you participate in acts against your convictions?
- Intentionally frighten you?
- Joke or make fun at your expense?
- Keep you isolated from your friends and/or family?
- Lie consistently?
- Make fun of your beliefs or education?
- Monitor your actions or behaviors?
- Neglect you?
- Prohibit friendships that you desire?
- Call you names or make fun of your weaknesses in general?
- Prohibit your further education of personal growth?
- Prohibit of restrict your use of a car or other mutual resources?
- Refuse to talk to you?

- Scold or rebuke you?
- Subject you to reckless driving?
- Threaten suicide?
- Threaten to commit you to a mental hospital?
- Threaten to destroy your belongings?
- Threaten to harm your children, family, or friends?
- Threaten to harm your pets?
- Threaten to have affairs?
- Threaten to lock you out of the house?
- Threaten to make you leave your own home?
- Threaten to report you to authorities?
- Threaten to take your children from you?
- Threaten to withhold money?
- Use weapons as a threat?
- Withhold approval or affection as punishment?
- Withhold counseling or therapy?

Physical Abuse

Does your partner...

- Attempt to choke, strangle, or suffocate you?
- Bite you?
- Break your bones?
- Bruise you?
- Burn or scald you?
- Confine you?
- Force you to dress in particular clothes?
- Harass you with unwanted tickling or touching?
- Harass you with unwanted visits or phone calls?
- Hit you or recklessly endanger you while you were pregnant?
- Hit you with a hand or an object?
- Hold you under water?
- Jolt or Shake you?
- Kick you? (Lissette 2000)

As I stated earlier in the book, Physical abuse is a criminal act.

It is a fact that 22%-35% of women's visits to the emergency room are related to domestic violence.

Social Abuse

Does your partner...

- Alienate you from your friends and family?
- Cause difficulties at your place of work?
- Control who can visit you, and when?
- Demand you move away from friends and supportive environments or people?
- Encourage friends who are abusive?
- Gossip or spread rumors about you?
- Insist you work at a job you dislike?
- Keep you imprisoned in your own home?
- Monitor your social activities?
- Refuse to let you work?
- Refuse to socialize with you or your friends?
- Tell secrets about you?
- Treat you disrespectfully in public?
- Try to get you fired from you job?
- Force you to kiss, touch or do other unwanted physical acts in public?
- Disclose personal matters or other acts to humiliate you in front of friends or family?

With adolescents, teenagers, and young adults, social abuse revolves more around the school environment involving friends, teachers, classmates, etc. (Lissette 2000)

Financial Abuse

Does your partner...

- Abuse credit cards by excessive spending?
- Force you into immoral acts for money?
- Incur excessive debts in your name?
- Intentionally default on loans as a control tactic?
- Involve you in illegal schemes for money?
- Keep your name off deeds, leases, or legal titles?
- Pawn your possessions?
- Refuse to include you in financial decisions?
- Refuse your access to jointly held funds or credit?
- Require you to ask permission to spend money?
- Restrict you to inadequate expense "allowances"?
- Use needed funds selfishly?
- Withhold available funds for necessary medical or dental care?
- Withhold child support payments?
- Withhold financial information?

(Lissette 2000)

Religious and Spiritual Abuse Inventory

Does your partner...

- Cite scripture out of context as a control tactic?
- Demand certain sexual conduct for spiritual or religious rituals?
- Destroy your religious objects or icons?
- Dictate your religious beliefs?
- Force you to participate in religious rituals?
- Force you to worship in a certain manner?
- Impose theology on you?
- Make fun of your beliefs or worship practices?

- Prohibit your spiritual or religious exploration?
- Take advantage of your forgiveness?

(Lissette 2000)

Sexual Abuse

Does your partner...

- Force you to have sex against your will (rape you)?
- Force unwanted sex acts, or perverted sex acts on you?
- Impose upon you that you must commit sex acts with other people and your partner?
- Force you to have oral or anal sex against your will?
- Demand that he be allowed to fondle or do other sex acts in public places?
- Use sexually explicit materials or force you to use pornography?
- Force you to be tied or restrained in any way while he performs sex?
- Use a knife, weapon, or another deadly threat while having sex?
- Take pictures of you that are sexually explicit against your will?
- Show friends and/or strangers pictures of you taken against your will?
- Have unprotected sex with other partners then with you without regard for disease?
- Use perverted language of sexual intent against you?
- Threaten to have an affair to coerce you?
- Threaten to violate a female child to force you to have sex?

(Lissette 2000)

These inventories are helpful in not only defining abuse, but also in identifying yourself in your relationship. These inventories are used to jog awareness. I must say, as I prepared materials for these writings, there were tactics of abuse that I had not even realized were subtle controls that had been used against me. Maybe you could add to the inventory lists or in an abusive relationship.

I'd like to thank Andrea Lissette for the useful appropriate quote from the late Dr. Martin Luther King, Jr., "Freedom is never voluntarily given by the oppressor; it must be demanded by the oppressed."

Please take a minute to say this prayer with me:

Lord, Thank you for forgiveness of all my sins.

Thank You for opening my eyes and ears to know what is true.

Thank You for strength to know what to do about the truth.

You word says, "...And they shall know the truth, and the truth shall set them free."

Thank You for saving me, Lord.

Thank You for filling me with Your Holy Spirit.

Give me the strength to demand my freedom from the oppressor, plan to implement it, and the grace to remain free.

In Jesus name, I pray, Amen.

CHAPTER 9
AND THE TRUTH SHALL
SET THEM FREE

Abuse happens to people of all ages, ethnic background, education, religion, etc. Many studies have been done of women survivors of domestic violence and results have shown very few commonalities among this group. This is not true with the abusers.

Feminists believe that looking for the cause of domestic violence by studying women is another form of victim blaming. According to reports, social learning theorists believe that female children who witness their mother's abuse are a higher risk for experiencing abuse themselves as they have a lower self esteem. Boys who also witness family violence are more likely as adults to abuse their partners than those boys from non-violent homes.

Here are some other interesting facts.

- Child abuse is 15 times more likely to occur in families where there is domestic violence.
- A child who witnesses domestic violence is highly at risk to become a juvenile delinquent and/or adult criminal.
- More than 3 million children witness acts of domestic violence each year.
- Acts of domestic violence occur every 15 seconds in the US.

- 20% of all murders in this country are committed within the family and 13% are committed by spouses.
- 22%-35% of all women who use the hospital emergency surgical service are battered.
- Each year, 6 million American women are beaten by their husbands or boyfriends. 4,000 die as a result.
- Battering is the single major cause of injury to women. **More frequent than automobile accidents, muggings, and rapes combined**.
- 1 in 4 female suicides are victims of family violence.

While you were reading these statistics, four women were severely beaten.

Characteristics of the abuser

Although abusers come from diverse backgrounds, as do victims of abuse, it has been noted that, young and old, abusers have very similar characteristics. All abusive individuals appear to possess a fundamental list of personality characteristics.

- Low self-esteem, though he may present himself otherwise to the outside world. This is one of the few characteristics that can be seen with most victims of abuse as well.
- Belief in male superiority and stereotyped masculine sex role in the family.
- Blames others for his actions. The abuser minimizes the impact of their violence and they redefine their behavior as something other than violence. They may emphasize loss of control and blame the victim for their behavior.
- Is pathologically jealous.
- Has dual personality, as noted time and time again from many personal accounts of abusive situations. Many women referred to their men as "Dr. Jekyll /

Mr. Hyde". This is another deceptive way a woman can get drawn back into a relationship i.e. she thinks that the abuser is only evil part of the time. She continues to hope that the nice man will return and give her a rest or reprieve. (This is the phase of calm in the cycle.)

- Has severe stress reactions; can't cope. He uses drinking and wife battering to cope.
- Frequently uses sex as an act of aggression to enhance self-esteem in view of waning virility; may be bi-sexual.
- Does not believe his violent behavior should have any consequences, after all, what he does is always someone else's fault. The abuser lives in denial.
- Extremely manipulative.
- Can be very charming.
- Some are very handsome. (Not all handsome men are abusers.)
- Some have criminal records (50%-80%)

The abuser is less likely to seek to break out of this state or the abusive cycles than the victims of abuse, unless the abuser receives therapy and accepts responsibility for his actions. The abuser is more likely to go out and find another victim of abuse.

The perception that the abusers have is that they are retaliating for attacks that they feel come from the wives or partners. The focus of the abuser is to regain control when actions of the victim are threatening to the abuser.

The abuser becomes dependent upon his partner not changing and maintaining her expected role in order to keep him in his superior position.

You can then realize the severity of the threat to the abuser when he sees his victim changing, striking independence, and breaking out of that fearful, immobile state that she was in.

It has long been a myth that all victims of abuse are the "same kind of people, with the same characteristics" as well. There are those who have endured abuse from childhood who, as in my own case, do fit this "textbook" example and perpetuate the life of a victim of abuse. However, the fact is that this is not the story for every victim of abuse. Fact also states, as indicated earlier, that any woman young and old, from all walks of life, can be a victim of abuse.

There is a great need to take a proactive approach in educating children regarding what the characteristics of safe people are, and by early intervention make an impact to stop the cycles of abuse in our children's lives.

We also have the need to warn children about the kinds of characteristics in people to "cut off" relations with or to "stay away" from in general, no matter how cute, popular, or envied this person might be. It is a known fact that many children have had their whole destiny altered by making a choice to have a relationship with the wrong type of character.

We need to continue to develop educational and training programs about domestic abuse for all medical, health, clinic/hospital law enforcement, community service agencies, churches, social service workers and school personnel. Health professionals and nursing staff as well as law enforcement (among those who were first trained) are now beginning to implement some training since the passing of the violence against women's act in 1994. Health service professionals and law enforcement workers are now encouraging individuals to seek support services when domestic violence is suspected.

What are some issues that children need to know?

1. Teach children there are appropriate ways of dealing with angry emotions.

2. Talk with youth about how they might get help dealing with anger at this time in their lives.

3. Children need to know they have value, no matter what they have been through, or what they still may go through.

4. Children need to know that they are not responsible for their parent's violence problems.

5. Children need to know that family violence is a crime. (For those of you who were not taught this as children, domestic violence is a CRIME!)

6. Children need to know appropriate assertive skills and how to protect themselves.

7. Children need to know that other people can help them. Children in an environment of violence often have difficulty knowing whom they can trust without causing themselves further pain and embarrassment.

8. Children can make a choice to not continue the cycle of abuse in their lives by getting help.

9. Children need to be taught about the various forms of abuse-physical, sexual, mental, emotional, etc. Date rape should also be highlighted with youth.

10. Children need to know that they have rights not to have to put up with any kind of abusive behavior-not at the home, or at school.

11. Children and the media need to be educated about the myths and facts regarding domestic violence. There are many myths, which have served to isolate the victims of abuse further in the past.

12. Children need to be told that there is a way that they should go when they grow older and domestic violence is not that way.

Since the topic of domestic violence is a new arena for education, this list will continue to grow.

Victims of domestic violence need to have the community reach out to them, and to be on the look out for them. Care needs to be taken while reaching out to someone in these circumstances, to ensure their safety at all times.

The victims of domestic violence need more trained advocates who are aware of how to proceed with caution when trying to help. Advocates need to simply show acceptance and love to someone who is abused. By reaching out several times and even relentlessly, if necessary, you may eventually gain the trust of a victim of violence. People who have lived through domestic violence have been hurt a lot and they learn to live in a survival mode. They are constantly on vigil, slow to trust someone new. Often, victims of abuse spend more time living and operating in the survival mode so that they and their children can stay alive than they do spending time making escape plans. The focus becomes, "I must make it through the day" rather that looking at a focus on "long term" plans of leaving the situation.

Why is it so cumbersome to a victim of domestic violence to think about leaving? If you carefully list all the risks that a woman faces when choosing to stay in a domestic violence situation and compare that list to all the risks she also faces when thinking about leaving the abuser, you will be amazed to see that the list for staying is nearly the same list as the one for leaving. The "leaving" list demonstrates a heightened risk and statistics show that the greatest number of abused women fatalities happen after the victim leaves. After realizing this, many would say, "Why on earth would a woman really make the move to leave?" As mechanical and surrealistic as this lifestyle can become, deep inside every woman knows that there is that possibility that she may wait too long to leave. As those statistics listed earlier clearly show, 4000 women a year have waited too long to leave, and they tragically did not survive.

Clearly, there is a need to identify all those elements that perpetuate domestic violence and develop effective methods to train our children and media that the cycle can stop with them. It is a choice. Everyone has to take a stand against violence. When we see something unfold in our communities that only serve to perpetuate the violence we need to be active on the town board and in our schools to stop the cycle of abuse. And we all need to pray for the innocent women and children that are still suffering.

We as a community and nation need to reach out to those who are stuck in a cycle of abuse, to those who have not been able to see a safe way or possible way to get out.

Maybe you know someone who is stuck in that state of immobility. Maybe that someone is you.

Please take a moment to pray this prayer with me:

Father God, Thank you for all that You have done for me.

Thank You for filling me with Your Spirit and for setting me free.

I cry out now for Your wisdom, direction, and strength that I need to make my own stand against violence and abuse.

Help me to set solid boundaries and moral standards, and by the Grace that only You can give me and help me to live up to those standards by the choices that I make for my life.

Let my choices be Godly choic.

In Jesus precious name, Amen.

CHAPTER 10
WHO ARE WE, REALLY?

When someone lives in an environment filled with immobility, shame, guilt, fear, and condemnation for a prolonged period of time, learned behaviors begin to emerge. Once our personality adopts these behaviors, we may become unable to react "normally" to demands of daily life.

A normal daily disagreement during the course of performing your job, at home, or other disappointments of life could be distorted to an unrealistic proportion by a person who has deep emotional wounds. A simple visit to the dentist office could remit unwanted emotions of anger or confusion, or could even leave the person feeling empty or rejected. These are examples that of course may not apply to everyone.

A woman who lives under the "thumb" of condemnation or abuse, in general learns that she is not allowed to voice her opinion or how she feels. The children growing up in this environment learn this lesson as well. The victim and the children are taught that you must "stuff" your emotions because speaking up for yourself only aggravates the abuser, causes more pain, and suffering. The victim learns that she will pay dearly for speaking up and therefore conforms to the submissive role, which encourages her not think, feel or speak (This is all true for the children living this way also).

The abuser is incredibly consistent and focused on his goal to not allow the victims to feel. It is my opinion that there are two major reasons for this phenomenon

> **Denial**: The abuser thinks that if he does not hear her speak her emotions, then it is like the abuse is not bothering her, maybe it's not even happening at all. The state of denial is reinforced with both the victim and the abuser.

> **Control**: The abuser is afraid of losing his control over the victim. If the abuser sees the victim becoming fearless to face the issues of what is going on and the abuser sees that he cannot impose fear upon the victim, the abuser begins to feel like he is losing control.

After years of this, a victim of abuse sustains deep emotional damage. It is important to know, that when someone is in deep emotional pain, a great amount of compassion and sensitivity is required in order for a counselor or an advocate to make a difference in their lives. It should be expected that a deeply wounded person can only focus on her own self. Until she can begin to heal, she may belabor issues. Be patient, this too will pass! If you are facing these painful emotional wounds yourself, again, this too shall pass.

It has been noted that hundreds of people recovering from loss or pain were asked;" What are the most productive methods of help?"(Out of their pain) It was clearly found that:

1. People wanted to be allowed to express how they feel, when they wanted to.

2. People wanted to be accepted and have their feelings accepted also.

3. People want to be with others who had shared similar experiences and who shared the same sense of loss.

In an abusive situation our normal process of learning how to "feel', express our emotions, and to react appropriately is distorted by an unhealthy pattern of thinking as described in earlier chapters. The truth is extremely therapeutic in dealing with the ups and downs of our challenges as long as that truth is administered in love. The reality is that many people seem to have difficulty knowing how to help people and they think they are helping by not saying anything, by not being truthful.

God's word says "Then you will know the truth, and the truth will set you free." (John 8:32). This is a biblical truth for the victim and it impacts on why the abuser does not want the victim to know the truth; so they will not be free.

It is important that in healing we realize that we must accept intense emotion. When we are at a place where we are most vulnerable we need to begin to face the truth daily.

The truth is, it is quite normal to be enraged if someone we love has been senselessly killed. It is also normal to feel despair when trying to restore equilibrium after someone you love has died. It is normal to feel intermittent vengeful anger or excitement after surviving a rape, abuse, assault, or serious injury or illness. Many people feel uncomfortable when hearing someone express intensely negative feelings. The fear is that the person may act out their feelings. Perhaps all they need is to vent these feelings. Of course, there is a greater need for consideration when a person does **nothing but** vent intense negativity. This **is not** "**O.K.**"

The initial part of the healing process for victims of abuse is to begin to identify, sort out, and direct those quite normal feelings and begin to learn a "new" way of reacting to everyday events that can be very painful to the wounded heart though not intentionally abusive. You learn to respond to these situations, rather than to react.

Renewal of our minds

After deliverance, which we have talked about in other chapters; the victims of abuse have many sutured wounds that are quite sensitive in the heart of that healing person. Though we no longer live in an abusive environment, we need to be able to learn to walk in our new way of thinking." Not everyone is calculating to abuse me or deceive me." In dealing with these old thinking patterns, we must look at how to identify and surrender shame, guilt, and condemnation.

In general, we need to learn how to continue to overcome and stay free from any other relationships that could be abusive.

Shame/Guilt

Let's talk first about shame. Shame and guilt are closely related, with guilt focusing on actions. For example, a person may feel guilty because he cheats or lies. Shame on the other hand focuses on personhood. Shame comes from feelings of unworthiness, failure, or nagging voice that says:" you're no good"! DeJong used an example of a football game. Going out of bounds would make a person feel guilty. Now if a person fails to reach the goal, that can bring that person to shame. Think of it this way: guilt comes when we go out of bounds or our boundaries and shame comes from failure to reach a goal we set within our own boundaries, set by things that we have learned to be acceptable. Those goals that we set for ourselves may be healthy or unhealthy goals. These goals may also be set within boundaries that are real or not real. Shame could be considered the swamp underneath the victim of abuse's guilt. One is capable of exacerbating the other unless deliverance and healing is seen. With either shame or guilt, there is a breech that obstructs the flow of God's love into a desperate life. Shame paralyzes deeply, even more deeply than feelings of punishment and rejection. Self-esteem is gone. The paralysis of shame can lead to hopelessness and even suicide if not surrendered and healed by God.

This is what the word of God says about shame:

Isaiah 54:4 says "Fear not, for thou shalt not be ashamed, neither be thou confounded, for thou shalt not be put to shame, for thou shalt forget the shame of thy youth, and shalt not remember the reproach of thy widowhood anymore."

This is very clear, but why do we find ourselves having shame oppress us? With cases of sexual abuse or any other kind of abuse, we can be left with shame.

Shame is defined as a painful feeling arising from the consciousness of something dishonorable done either by self or someone else to you. God's word is also very clear to direct us to all issues that can bring shame upon us. Of course, I have now learned to resist shame. It cannot become a thief in my life. I choose to resist the effects and issues that shame can bring. I have learned that no matter what

man can do to me, God, through the blood of Jesus-
has put honor on me and no man can take it away!

In searching the scriptures, here is a list of things
that can bring shame: (not an exhaustive list):

1. People that hate us. (Psalms 44:7)

2. Those that seek after my soul to destroy and
    wish me evil. (Psalms 40:14,15)

3. To leave a child to himself. (Proverbs 29:15)

4. To speak or answer before he hears what is
    said. (Proverbs 18:13)

5. Those that seek my hurt shall be brought to
    shame. (Psalms 71:24)

6. Faces filled with shame that they may seek
    thy name, oh, Lord. (Psalms 83:16)

7. Pride. (Proverbs 11:2)

8. Rebuking a mocker or contemptuous person
    (Proverbs 9:1)

9. To be a fool. (Proverbs 3:35)

10. Son that causes shame and brings reproach
    (Proverbs 19:26)

11. Wicked man is loathsome, wicked cometh to
    shame. (Proverbs 13:5)

12. Shame brings confusion. (Isaiah 30:3,
    Psalms 109:29)

Scripture refers to shame bringing confusion. This is interesting when we realize that shame is a major tool used by the abuser against his victim. He uses shame as long as the victim will believe the lies that shame brings. The more shame, the more confusion comes upon the victim. The confusion then, places a greater bondage on the victim. The atmosphere of confusion perpetuates the immobility or inability to function normally. Those that can choose to repent and renounce the shame and the many reactions that go with shame i.e. confusion, fear, reproach, pride, disobedience, depression, neglecting a child or leaving him to himself, and suicide can overcome shame. Walk away and stay away from the bondage to these things.

Guilt

Please review Chapter 2 where I spoke about guilt. This will expand on what has been outlined in that chapter. Guilt is another method of keeping the victim of abuse in bondage, it is used so much in breaking down the character in a victim of domestic violence that it, also needs to be addressed seriously. Guilt is an area that needs to be renounced. As indicated above any of the other bondages that have come as a result of guilt should also be repented of and surrendered to God.

Overcoming

Overcoming is a transition in mind, soul, spirit, and body from a victim mentality to the victor mentality. I wish I could say that this was a quick process, but it is not unless the sovereign hand of God intervenes. I also wish that I could say that it was easy-but it was not.

.   Let's look at what God's word says about overcoming. God's word clearly states what we will gain by overcoming and what we need to do to overcome. These instructions are too important for our present and future freedom not to share in the context of this book.

A powerful story of overcoming comes from Numbers chapter 13 and 14. Numbers 14:30 says, "And Caleb stilled the people before Moses and said; 'Let us go up at once and possess it, for we are **well able to** overcome it.'" Caleb had a vision that was built on **faith**.

Instead of having faith along with Joshua and Caleb, the Israelites; who had been delivered from Egypt, murmured and complained against Moses and Aaron. Moses had led the Israelites by the hand of God to the Jordan River on the border of the Promised Land. Moses had sent spies into the Promised Land who brought back grapes, pomegranates and figs. The spies said, "Surely this land flows with milk and honey", but those in the congregation of the Israelites were afraid of the

Amalikites, the Hittites, Jebusites, and the Canaanites (This could be another whole chapter).

God had made a solemn promise to the nation Israel. The existence of a remnant is necessary to uphold the integrity of God who has every intention of fulfilling His promises. Throughout history in the bible, God dealt with a believing remnant: Caleb and Joshua (Numbers13, 14); Noah, (Genesis 6:5-9), Deborah and Barah, (Judges 4); Gideon, (Judges 7); Samson, (Judges 13-17), Samuel, (1Sam2); and many others. I was reflecting on why some of the bazaar stories we read about took place at all. I felt as if God whispered to me "my voice needs to be heard, and obeyed". There will be no set pattern by which we can learn to walk out our own faith other than to hear and obey the voice of God. In I John 5:4, we read: "For whosoever is born of God overcomes the world and this is the victory that overcomes the world, even our faith." There is an absolute need for God's promises to be fulfilled through a generation that is solid in their faith.

Faith is the key to overcoming. We know that faith comes by hearing and hearing by the word of God. I believe that Caleb saw and heard from God, which built up his faith to overcome. Caleb believed "Whatever is over there, we are able to overcome it!"

In earlier chapters I spoke of a faith that welled up inside of me that I finally knew that no

matter what has happened already or what was yet
to come-I had faith that God was there for me to
deliver us out of the pit of domestic violence-this
was the Caleb-kind of faith! I had one great big
Hittite to distract me from what God had spoken,
but I kept my focus on what God said and just
waited for the fruition of what He had said to
happen safely in our lives.

Another element necessary to overcome is to
be in God's peace and to be of good cheer. In John
16:33 it says, "These things I have spoken unto you,
that in me you might have peace. In the world you
shall have tribulation: but be of good cheer, I have
overcome the world." If we rest in God's peace that
the work is finished, we can be of good cheer
despite what we go through, or how difficult it is.

In many verses, depending on the
translation, overcome is used interchangeably with
"stand". It is very important that we stand firm in
God's armor and God will "stand" for us against the
evil in the world.

What is God's armor? We need to memorize
and quote scripture against the attacks of the devil.
When we do speak the word of God over a situation
we are empowering our God to work on our behalf
in any given situation. Jesus is the word made flesh.
He is a living God Who is activated when we speak
His word. By doing so it is like putting on a suit of
armor daily! In Ephesians 6:13-17 It states,
"Wherefore take unto you the whole armor of God,

that You may be able to withstand (overcome) in
the evil day, and having done all, to stand; stand,
therefore, having your loins girt about with the
truth, and having on the breastplate of righteousness
and your feet shod with the preparation of the
gospel of peace. Above all, taking the shield of
faith, wherewith you will be able quench all the
fiery darts (attacks) of the wicked, and take the
helmet of salvation, and the helmet of salvation and
the sword the sword of the spirit, which is the word
of God." (Important enough to quote 2xx).

To someone who has never been aware, the
battle that we fight is not a flesh and blood battle.
Rather, we fight in the spirit realm against
principalities, against powers, against rulers of
darkness of this world, against spiritual wickedness
in high places. (Ephesians 6:12) If this is new
information to you, then you are probably laughing
out loud at this point. Let me tell you, I had to learn
the hard way-as I had mentioned in earlier chapters,
many years of my life were robbed, many dreams
shattered, my children were put at risk, I nearly lost
my life and I did lose the life of my firstborn baby
girl. We desperately need the Lord Jesus to fight for
us! These might be strange scriptural thoughts, but
the more God reveals the truth of this word to you
(and He will if you ask Him!), the more you will
cling to what God says to do in this scripture in
order to overcome.

Another important point we need in order to
overcome is to know who we are in Christ. Even
after you thought you were free and healed, people
who are recovering from abuse can be tempted to
fall back into shameful thinking patterns. Such
thoughts as we have talked about, are not of God.
You speak the word against those thoughts. We
need to stay clean of these old bondages that is to
stand in your freedom by knowing that we are the
righteousness of Christ and further to work hard to
walk in that righteousness. I John 4:4 states: "Ye are
of God, little children, and have overcome them,
because greater is He who is in you than he who is
in the world."(The worldly "he" is the devil)." In
Revelation 17:14 it says, "These shall make war
with the lamb and the lamb shall overcome them for
He is the Lord of Lord's, the King of Kings and
they that are with Him are called chosen and
faithful." We that stand firm in our faith are called
chosen and faithful.

II Corinthians 5:21 states "For He hath made Him
to be sin for us, who knew no sin; that we might be
made the righteousness of God in Him. We can
remain expectant of our Father when we know who
we are in Him. "Do not be overcome by evil, but
overcome evil with good." Romans 12:21. God can
work every bit of power, miraculously through us as
long as we stay in God's love in everything we do.
This is extremely hard after living in an abusive
situation. You see, God is love; any sin that comes

to stop the flow of God's love needs to be repented of so that we can walk in the fullness of God's love. The power and love of God will then freely flow through us as clean pure vessels. We need to walk in every bit of the power that God says he has given us in order to usher in His kingdom on earth. We cannot do that when we allow sin to overcome us Keep a careful watch and stand against old shameful thinking.

God also says that He will give us a new name. (Rev.2: 17) "He that overcomes I will make a pillar in the temple of God, and he shall go no more out and I will write upon him the name of God, and the name of the city of my God, which is the New Jerusalem, which cometh down out of heaven from my God, and I will write upon him my new name." Revelation 3:12. That's awesome! God tells us that we are blessed, we are His righteousness, we are prosperous, and the works that He did we will do also.

A dear mentor and prayer warrior had a favorite expression: "When the devil tries to threaten you about who you are and what your future is, you remind him of how he was defeated and that he has no future!"

Another key to overcoming is to pray. Listen to the voice of God and obey what He says to do. "He that hath ears to hear, let him hear what the spirit says to the churches. To him that overcomes will I give of the tree of life which is in the midst of the paradise of God". Revelation 2:7.

God had given me a vision of myself climbing up to a higher level in the spirit realm. (I also believe this was prophetic for the church.) This was the way it had appeared in the vision, I saw a high ledge in front of the sanctuary of our church, where the alter is. There was a river of water flowing over the ledge. At first I was outside the sanctuary trying to get others to go inside the sanctuary, then finally, I felt an urgency in me to just go in myself. I ran to the alter area and I pulled myself up on to the ledge with the water flowing over me, when I reached the top and stood up, a mighty rushing wind hit me and I remember blowing over like a reed in the wind, my feet were anchored in the rock-like ledge, thank God, I did not blow away, my feet were not moving, solid on the rock. God wants to plant our feet in the solid rock of Jesus. "And I say unto you, that you art Peter, and upon this rock I will build my church; the gates of hell shall not prevail against it." Matt.16:18 Once we as a church are planted, firmly on the rock of Jesus and His word, (which are one), when the wind of the Holy Spirit blows, we will bend with obedience everywhere the wind blows. Likewise, when the wind of adversity blows upon us, we will not be blown away or crushed. God is building a glorious church filled with obedient children. We will overcome!

Please take a moment to pray this prayer with me:

Dear Father in Heaven, Thank you that greater is He who is in me than he who is in the world.

You have already completed the work so that I can be the overcomer.

Thank you that I can surrender all fears doubts, frustrations, anger, bitterness, shame and guilt to you.

I take back all authority I have given to the devil through holding on to any of these things that I have surrendered to you, I choose to give all authority back to my Lord Jesus Christ.

I break the yoke of all these listed things (bitterness, fears, etc.)

I bind and rebuke all these things in the name of Jesus.

Holy Spirit come and fill me up with your power.

Thank You for emotional healing in Jesus name.

Thank you for continued strength to overcome daily in my walk of faith with you.

In Jesus Name, Amen.

CHAPTER 11
IN AS MUCH AS YOU'VE DONE IT

We have talked about the impact that abuse in general has on the victim. A type of abuse that bores deep emotional wounds and scars on the heart and spirit of the victim is sexual abuse.

In reading about domestic violence, it may be overlooked at times how traumatic it is to be forced to have sexual relations with someone who emotionally degrades you, physically abuses you, destroys your property, robs you and works to keep you in bondage. Sexual activity is not associated with love in these kinds of circumstances. In fact, the victim learns a perverted type of love, a very unnatural type of love.

Often, the woman in bondage to an abusive partner (who forces her to do sexual acts that she is not comfortable with) becomes terrorized-even like a young child who is being victimized by a perpetrator. As mentioned earlier, the victim learns to perpetuate an unhealthy, unbalanced, shameful kind of understanding of what love really is. This kind of love is perverted and certainly not the way God intended for a man to love a woman or for a woman to be loved. This is why pornography is so destructive to a relationship. It has been referred to as "woman hate" by domestic violence advocates. Pornography has been determined as a common problem with many men who have resorted to violent crimes against women such as rape and murder. Pornography degrades the normal sense of "family" or respect for women, not to ignore the perversion it promotes in those lives that have been drawn into an addiction of the use of it.

The marriage bed was considered so sacred for many years that it was thought that it was no one else's business what went on in the bedroom. When there is domestic violence, often the woman is forced to do sexual things that she does not want to do. As mentioned earlier the act alone may be offensive to a victim of abuse. If a man sexually forces himself on a woman, whether married or not this is still considered "rape".

According to Intimate Betrayal (Wiehe, Richards 1995) rape is defined as any sexual activity that one experiences without giving consent. This may include fondling, oral, anal, or vaginal intercourse or other unwanted sexual activity. If both parties do not consent to the sexual activity then the act becomes a violation of the privacy and dignity of the individual who is the target or victim. This is true even if the individuals involved know each other. (Wiehe, Richard, 1995) Repeated, violent sexual acts against a victim of domestic violence only serve to wound the victim of violence more deeply.

Often abusers use sexual perversion and abuse as a way to gain more control over the victim. The victim of abuse will often become more

confused after having these acts performed whether
against her will or not. The victim struggles hard
emotionally to make sense out of the contradictions
that go on with this sick kind of "love".

The abuser will also use sex as a "twisted"
kind of peace offering after a violent episode. He
may say he is sorry 100 times for recklessly
endangering the whole family and promise that he
will never do it again while he sweetly caresses his
victim-this tactic is also a means of control over the
victim. This method of manipulation numbs the
victim back into a state of denial and confusion.
Thoughts such as "maybe he didn't mean to do
what he did', reinforces the victim's immobile state,
ensures that she will not try to escape. Many times
the victim will begin to think that it is her fault that
she is unable to please him sexually, so he has to
resort to some of the perverted things that he does to
be satisfied, including abuse. **Of course, this is far
from the truth**. Some abusers reinforce this pattern
of thinking by belittling the victim while he is
having his way with her-further wounding her
emotionally.

It is important to know that these acts that
are committed against your will really have nothing
to do with you. These things have nothing to do
with the real, true "inside" you that God intended
you to be. The reasons for the abuse lie with the
abuser's perversions and problems-not with the
victim (Morrison, A Safe Place"). Immoral, violent

acts against your body cannot make you someone you are not. Unfortunately, many of us swallow this lie that "so and so made me this way, my life is ruined, no one will ever want to love me now, etc. etc."

In earlier chapters, we talked about shame, guilt, and overcoming. Shame and guilt become a belief system accompanied by unhealthy thinking patterns within the victim's mind. You tend to begin by accepting a few lies about yourself, then before you can even realize what is going on, almost all of your thinking can become based on shame or guilt or some other unhealthy emotion such as anger, bitterness, or self rejection.

Of course, it becomes very hard not to find justification for your shame, guilt, etc. when the cycle of events serve to perpetuate that shame-when the cycle of events finds justification for the guilt. Maybe it is very easy to perpetuate that anger or bitterness because of everything that unjustly happens to you.

You know you are being used and sexually, emotionally abused yet you feel it would be more dangerous for you to try to leave the abusive situation. You become quite used to looking for ways that may be less painful but you wind up between a "rock and a hard place" with all that you attempt to do. You become hurt, angry, and hateful toward the perpetrator. In some cases (as in my case), the emotions are so wounded, hidden, that you become angry with everyone around you. It is difficult to trust anyone you come in contact with.

I hadn't realized myself that I was also experiencing many of those emotional responses seen with victims of "stranger rape". It has been a popular opinion that the more serious type of rape is rape from a stranger. Over the years, it has become more evident that wounds go very deep when the rape comes from a person known and trusted by the victims.

Rape or other violent sexual assaults on the survivor of the abuse leaves a scar on the emotions of the victims. Whether the victim knows the rapist, as in domestic partner situation or not; studies show that both groups scored similarly on measures of depression, anxiety, quality of subsequent relationships, and sexual satisfaction following the rape. (Wiehe, Richards, 1995).

Other areas that affected the survivors of rape are the ability to trust others, the ability to be intimate with others and the ability to deal with their anger experienced in response to the rape.

With God's help, through deliverance, prayer, counseling and group or individual therapy, victims of sexual abuse can learn to trust others again. They can also learn as discussed already, to begin to use healthy thinking patterns, thoughts that are first pure gentle, etc. Not everyone wants to abuse you!

Survivors need to learn how to identify when a painful memory is ruling their ability to trust. For example, there are certain events in life that may "trigger" a flashback or painful memory. Some triggers might be a familiar smell in the air, seasons, and actions that a survivor or significant person may do. Familiar sites, tastes, objects or even seeing someone who is the same age that you were when the trauma occurred could also set off triggers. This is especially true with age if abuse took place while a child, you can add to this list of triggers if you wish. Once the survivors begin to allow healing, they can become aware and recognize what is happening to them when a painful memory is triggered. They can get whatever help they need when a painful memory surfaces. These are also the types of responses seen with victims of post-traumatic stress syndrome.

Steps can be taken to slowly work through the pain "that's right, that was the past, no one is calculating to hurt me now, if someone does hurt me it's not like before, I am moving forward now and not everyone hurts with intentions to abuse". (Don't forget there will be many people who will hurt you or disappoint you, this is a part of life a simple example is the dentist). You begin to encourage yourself with what is true in the situation.

In my own personal case, it was so difficult for me to trust people that the only way I could begin to take baby steps to trust, was to pray to God to give me strength to learn to trust. My only hope was to trust in my God that no one could hurt me anymore and if I was hurt, the wisdom to forgive quickly. I knew that in order to grow and heal I had to learn to trust other people. This was a very hard thing for me to do. I learned how to trust God so that I could trust other people and I prayed for God to give me discernment to deal with circumstances that I may encounter. I also prayed that God would keep my spiritual eyes open so that I could see deception coming. I still walk this walk everyday. I wish I could say I have passed all the tests, but I have had a few retakes. Even though you are delivered and a new creature, you need to daily stand your ground against the temptations of the flesh and taunts of the enemy.

You may be thinking that is a bit much- when do you find any peace? The fact is the battle becomes easier when you give the fight over to God completely. You need to forfeit your fleshly desires to retaliate when you're hurt or angry, forfeiting the natural desire to satisfy that inner urge to live by your emotions. As Pastor says, "Respond, don't react to situations."

FIND YOUR PEACE IN GOD! Though men may be the vessels used to do God's work, it is not of God to fear men.

Know also, that men are human and will let
you down but God will never fail you! Now if you
are still dealing with anger toward God, then maybe
it's time to renounce a few things and get your heart
right with God. He is all you've got to go with!
Every other creature and thing is sure to disappoint
you at one time or another. Maybe you are saying,
"I am sunk then. I am feeling far away from God
and all men are sure to disappoint me-where am I
going? Well, you want to survive, so you are going
to take baby steps toward God. You may feel far
away from Him but He is never far from you! Talk
to Him daily about how you feel, read His word and
counsel with someone who is strong in their faith
and can pray with you until you breakthrough! Tell
God you choose to forgive Him and ask Him to
forgive you for not trusting in Him. You will find
your peace that only God can give. In Psalm 26:3 it
says, Thou wilt keep him in perfect peace, whose
mind is stayed on thee: because he trusts in thee."
Psalm 28:7 says "The Lord is my strength and my
shield; my heart trusts in Him, and I am helped:
therefore my heart greatly rejoices and with my
song I will praise Him." Psalm 29:11 "The Lord
will give strength unto His people; the Lord will
bless His people with peace." Luke 1:79 clearly
states" To give light to them that sit in darkness and
in the shadow of death, to guide our feet into the
way of peace." All of these words are so filled with
life!

One has to realize that our God, who knows us better than anyone else-also knew the need to instill peace unto His children and also the need to encourage us to keep our trust in the author and the finisher of our faith-that is Christ Jesus, our Lord.

"Who shall separate us from the love of Christ?" (Romans 8:35) Abuse of any kind, be it physical, emotional, spiritual, sexual, and financial or otherwise is a perversion of God's love. It is the devil's attempt to destroy our faith in Christ and therefore destroy our witness, peace and salvation in Christ. I HAVE REALLY GOOD NEWS!!! The end of my favorite scripture is found in Romans 8:35-39 and reads: "shall tribulation, or distress, or persecution, or famine, or nakedness, or peril, or sword? As it is written, for thy sake we are killed all the day long, we are accounted as sheep for the slaughter. Nay, in all these things we are more than conquerors through Him that loved us. For I am persuaded that neither death, nor life, nor angels, nor principalities, nor powers, nor things present, nor things yet to come. Nor height, nor depth, nor any other creature, shall be able to separate us from the love of God, which is in Christ Jesus our Lord!" Thank you God!

Please take a moment to pray this prayer with me:

Dear Father in heaven, when I was broken, You picked me up, brushed me off and held me close to

You until my pain could not stay within me anymore.

It had to be taken by You, as Your word is true that nothing shall be able to separate me from the love of God.

You saw everything, and you never stopped loving me, not once.

Forgive me, oh my God, if I have blamed You for my pain or if I have held onto anger because of the sexual abuse.

Forgive me for being angry with others including the abuser. I choose to forgive all who have hurt me. I take back every bit of authority I gave to the devil through my anger against You first, then also from anger I felt toward others.

I choose to give that authority back to my Lord Jesus Christ.

Now, I break the yoke of those spirits of anger and unforgiveness, in Jesus name.

I bind you spirits of anger and unforgiveness, in the name of Jesus Christ and I command you to leave me alone, right now in Jesus name.

Holy Spirit come in to my life completely fill every area of my body with Your Holy presence.

Fill me to over flowing with a love that only you can give to me.

Thank you Jesus for complete peace and for comforting me. I pray for a spiritual, mental, emotional, physical, moral, and financial hedge of protection over myself and all of my family members.

In Jesus precious name. Amen.

CHAPTER 12

WHAT ABOUT THE CHILDREN?

What about the children? Much is written about battered women, domestic partner abuse, and violence against women. I am grateful to see what was denied, buried, and hidden for so many years finally come to a public light. In 1994, the Violence Against Women Act was passed to make a political statement that violence against women is a violation of women's civil rights. Thank You God, for this progress!! Still, in the back of my mind looms the question, what about the children? What about the innocence that was robbed from them at an early age? What about the fear that gripped them early on? It will be with them until God is able to liberate their innocent lives of the secret family violence.

In many cases, where there is domestic violence, there is the high risk factor that the children will be personally, directly, physically, and sexually abused. When family security is violated in this way, childhood as it is meant to be by God comes to a screeching halt. For example, one day the boy or girl is 5, 6, 7, or 8 years old-the next day, they are 18 years old, finding themselves under mental, physical, emotional, and moral pressures way beyond what they are capable of handling.

They are unaware of how to stop or how to cope with their pain, guilt, and fear.

It is also a very shameful family situation. Children do not dare invite their friends over to visit, nor do they feel it is o.k. to talk freely with anyone about all the pressures that they experience emotionally.

How do you cover the shame you live in and act "normal" at school? Many people will put you down "just for looking at them". Peer pressure is brutal in the school systems.

So much of what a child from this type of background has been taught is, you need to survive, and you can't afford to be a child. You might wind up dead.

You also see that children gain a twisted ability to love other people. They gain a crash course on sexuality, especially where sexual abuse is involved with the child. There was a case where a woman with six children killed her sexually and physically abusive husband. He had already violated one of the daughters and threatened to have sex with the youngest daughter in front of the wife. This was a means of manipulating her. She killed him to prevent him from doing this. This type of family violence is common in the domestic violence environment. The fact is, everyone needs to be 5, 6, 7, 8, 9, and 10 years of age. It is important to be able to live an innocent childhood. Children in homes of physical and sexual abuse and violence have their childhood stolen from them by force.

In most cases, children who have been sexually and/ or physically abused lose their security, peace, and comfort. As a result, they have a direct hit in the area of learning and growing because the normal developmental process has been interrupted.

Everything that was just mentioned is vital in order to create an ability in the child to trust other adults. It has been said that when trust is broken, childhood dies. When this death of the childhood occurs, suddenly as a child you know more about pain, guilt, shame and sex than anyone at this young age should know. (Morrison, Safe Place)

What is worse is the hindered emotional development. It is now at a level where it is not a good coping ground for the child, unable to cope with even the slightest setback. Many children cannot even mourn the loss of their childhood. They have to "suck it up" and become like a stone so that they can continue to survive.

In A Safe Place by Jan Morrison, she reviews all these aspects of mourning the loss of childhood. She said that it is impossible to accept the full truth about your abuse until you mourn the loss of the child who died believing the lies. (A reference about sexual abuse.)

I believe, having watched my children grow up before their time, that these facts are also true with children who are emotionally and fearfully traumatized through watching years of domestic violence.

Just a reflection of my personal account. After years of living in "Hell", my children's lives had been jeopardized for the last time, when the perpetrator did $5,835.00 of damage on the house right in front of them.

My son reported his father to the State Police, because this took place in my absence. The kids had after school activities cancelled and had come home on the bus. My daughter called me from the neighbor's house and told me to get home quickly.

After this criminal event the perpetrator was on a registry for child abuse, and yet he was able to drag us to court repeatedly trying to gain unsupervised visitation. As mentioned earlier, I was going to court on a weekly basis at one point. The abuser was petitioning from the county jail trying to secure a court mandate that the kids came to see him in jail. The children had simply had enough. How much more of their lives would be robbed? They still need to mourn the loss of their innocence, their childlike comfortable place that was violated. It was not their fault.

People mourn their losses in different ways; some cry, some get angry. It is important to acknowledge your hurt. It is normal to be angry about what has happened to you. You just need to learn not to stay in anger and generalize the anger to other people, yourself, or circumstances. Some people work relentlessly to attempt to make life the way it was before the abuse or to make it the way they want it to be. They also want to find the children that they once were and "fix" the world for themselves. Some pretend that they haven't lost anything, so we don't need to mourn, according to Jan Morrison.

As I have repeated in earlier chapters, I truly am convinced that the problem of domestic violence needs to be stopped with our precious youth. I was speaking at a youth group about violence and a 13-year-old girl said to me, "Where is our safe place to be anymore?" She went on to say it used to be safe to go to school, and safe at home. She said this isn't true anymore.

Children need to know that they can be safe and feel secure. As a society, we directly see an impact on a generation such as these precious ones. They are growing up struggling with an ability to trust the adult makers of the world. Their lives have been turned upside down living in a generation filled with latch key kids, single parent homes, or no "present parents". We as a society need to encourage our youth and educate them about perpetrators of violence i.e. future abusers, rapists, or manipulators.

Our children need to know that no matter where they have come from or what their experiences, that each one of them is a chosen vessel of God. They need to know that God created them from before the foundation of the earth, for His good purpose. Each young person is beautiful, precious, and very valuable. They might not believe it now, but we need to begin to educate them in ways to allow them to be treated well, without apologizing for it. They need to know what is the intended way that love should be introduced, not as sex or manipulation or through other perversions. They need to know that in Romans 8:28, God says, "And we know that all things work together for good to them that love God, and are called according to His purpose." In this verse, there are two key parts in reference to the youth.

1. Know. They can't know unless the ones who do know teach them. Children from violent homes have no idea that their lives can work together for any "good".

2. "To them who are called according to His purpose." God called every one of us to fulfill the destiny that He has placed on our lives.

Many times, choices that are made at a young age change the course of a destiny. For example, the 13 year old who becomes pregnant has her first child at 13, possibly a second at 14 years old, and a third at 17 years old all the time tries to grow up emotionally and is still stuck at an emotional age of nine.

Or- the healthy, solid sixteen year old, who was great in school, on honor society, cheerleader, with no history of violence becomes involved with a bully type handsome football player who possesses her and manipulates her until she drops everything including school. When this low point brought her to a decision to break up with him, he killed her and put her in the trunk of his car. (Extreme, but true).

"Train up a child in the way he should go, and when he is old, he will not depart from it." (Proverbs 22:6) Children who are from broken backgrounds are even more at risk but this verse is true for all our youth. Here is a scripture that speaks clearly to me that some order exists in what is known or expected to be "normal". I Corinthians 13:11: "When I was a child, I spoke as a child, I understood as a child, I thought as a child. But when I became a man, I put away childish things." It seems to say to me that to develop otherwise whether it be emotionally or even spiritually-would be contrary to the word of God. It would say there is a time and a season to be a man. When things in our lives happen to pervert the way things should be naturally, I believe there is an impact on the spiritual and moral part of our inner man. Teaching is a way to restore the things that need to be restored, and so are prayer, deliverance, and the mercy and grace of God on the lives of our youth.

Violence in the home should only be referred to as "battered women" when there are "no children" in the homes to be impacted by this environment.

A report from an agency representative of a youth program has said that 75% of the runaway youth were running from domestic violence. A large percentage of the homeless population is women and children running from a violent partner or perpetrator.

The court systems need to develop effective ways to evaluate an abusive perpetrator when history has been clearly documented. It is further abuse to the women and children involved to allow the abuser to repeatedly drag the family into court. This is damaging emotionally to the women and children and financially devastating to a family who is already on a single parent income.

What is more valuable, to allow healing in the children and women and to set up programs to therapeutically address the abuser's problems or to continue to allow the family to be abused by the abuser-only through a new channel (the court system)? (Stats. for rehabilitation for the abuser have not proven to be beneficial at this point.)

Forced reconciliation during custody/visitation trials in civil court is a common reason that abused women and children do end up back in the grips of their abuser. The women see that the system is not helping them, so they buckle under and everyone suffers in the long run.

The system needs to see the manipulative, controlling tactics of the abuser for what they really are, as it comes to delivery of fair hearing legislation. The children need our protection and education. They are our future adults! Will we begin to train a new breed or will those who have lived under the training of domestic violence perpetuate that violence? I believe we need to actively address this issue of violence in our school systems for the sake of the health of our future society.

Please join in with me in this prayer:

Father, forgive us as a society for the neglect of our children in the past.

Forgive us for not training them up in the way that they should go.

Forgive me for the state that my own children are in.

Send Your mercy and grace upon our lives, and take away any condemnation.

Assist us in knowing the right way to deal with the issues of our children's needs.

I come against rebellion and other witchcraft spirits that have come to rob our children.

I bind these spiritual forces in Jesus name.

Please direct each of us in the decisions we need to make in the future, and we repent of decisions that have not rendered good in the lives of our children.

Heal their pain.

I cancel every assignment that the devil has against my children in Jesus name.

Bless them, open up their spiritual eyes and ears to see and hear how valuable they are to You, Lord, and how precious.

You created them to be full of destiny on this earth.

We claim our children's lives for the kingdom of God and Thank You, Lord, for their liberty, blessings, and good success.

In Jesus name I pray, Amen

This is a good prayer for the youth of the nation, if you do not have your own children.

AND THE POWER AND GLORY FOREVER, AMEN.

CONCLUSION

Baby Steps

There are important steps that we need to walk through. I wish that there was an instant transformation that could evolve us for a moment of safety and we would never have to fight in court, or struggle to stay free from the abuser. The truth is, you need to decide what you are going to do. I want to encourage you to make a plan, find supports, and then stand firm. Keep your focus and get free by walking through each brave step.

My pastor preached an excellent message filled with comfort in the wake of the Twin Tower tragedy in New York City. He told the congregation that our God has a secret place for each of us to hide. Although Pastor was feeding his sheep words of comfort and strength in light of the terror that struck our great nation, these words of comfort ring true for those in terror of their own safety daily in their homes.

I spoke at the "Take back the night" rally and made a point that terror is terror and violence is violence. Only God is our refuge in times when tyranny threatens to control us as individuals or as a nation.

What is the secret place that God provides for us? My Pastor stressed that:

1. God hides us in a secret place when we are in the House of God. So, if you don't already have a church family, pray and God will direct you to a secret place where you can be fed by a good pastor and join a spiritual family.

2. God hides us in a secret place of His presence. People who walk out the walk of escaping domestic violence need to know a God who is real by getting closer to Him and knowing His presence. God's word says, "In His presence, there is fullness of joy."

3. God hides us in a secret place through praise and worship and prayer in His Holy name. Psalms 16:11 "You will show me the path of life; in Your presence is fullness of joy and at Your right hand there are pleasures forever more."

Even before I had a clue, God drew me through praise and worship. I became stronger and clearer in thought. God happened to use praise and worship and prayer as the times that He would speak to me the most. I would not fear anything in His presence, in His church, singing and praying to Him. You need to call to the name of the Lord Jesus Christ to keep your feet directed in the way you need to go.

Here are some scriptural promises brought out by Pastor's sermon on 9/30/01 that will keep you in perfect peace and comfort you daily as you make each courageous step count. Read these verses, recite them and stand firm that God is your fortress and refuge. He is your warrior walking with you through each difficult moment in time.

Psalms 91:1 – 16

"He that dwells in the secret place of the most high shall abide under the shadow of the Almighty. I will say of the Lord, He is my refuge and my fortress: my God in Him I will trust. Surely He shall deliver you from the snare of the fowler and from the pestilence. He shall cover you with His feathers, and under His wings shall you trust. His truth shall be your shield and buckle. You shall not be afraid for the terror by night, or for the arrow that flies by day. Nor for the pestilence that walks in darkness, nor for the destruction that wastes at noonday. A thousand shall fall at your side and ten thousand at your right hand, but it shall not come nigh thee. Only with thine eyes shall you behold and see the reward of the wicked because you have made the Lord, which is my refuge, even the most high, my habitation. There shall no evil befall thee, neither shall any plague. Come nigh your dwelling. For He shall give His angels charge over you to keep you in all your ways. They shall bear you up in their hands, lest you dash your foot against a stone. You shall tread upon the lion and adder, the young lion and the dragon shall you trample under feet because He has set His love upon me. Therefore will I deliver Him. I will set Him on high, because He hath known my name. He shall call upon me, and I will answer Him. I will be with and honor Him. With long life will I satisfy Him, and show Him my salvation." This is one of my most favorite collections of scriptures.

Psalms 46:1 – 8

God is our refuge and strength, a very present help in time of trouble. Therefore will not we fear, though the earth is removed, and though the mountains are carried into the midst of the sea. Though the waters thereof roar and be troubled, though the mountains shake with the swelling thereof. There is a river of streams whereof shall make glad the city of God, the Holy place of the tabernacles of the most high. God is in the midst of her, she shall not be moved: God shall help her and that right early. The heathen raged, the kingdoms were moved; He uttered His voice, the earth melted. The Lord of Hosts is with us, the God of Jacob is our refuge. Come behold the works of the Lord. What desolations he hath made in the earth.

Psalms 31:19 – 20

Oh how great is thy goodness, which thou hast laid up for them that fear thee, which thou hast wrought for them that trust in thee before the sons of men!

AND THE POWER AND GLORY FOREVER, AMEN.

Hebrews 10:25

Not forsaking the assembling of ourselves together, as the manner of some is but exhorting one another and so much the more as ye see the day approaching.

Psalms 32:6 – 7

For this shall everyone that is godly pray unto thee in a time when thou may be found: surely in the floods of great waters they stall not come nigh unto Him. Thou art my hiding place. Thou shall preserve me from trouble. Thou shall compass me about with songs of deliverance.

      Statistics change constantly as the various elements of our society changes. Here are some statistical facts that are interesting at this point in time:

- "Women's greatest risk of violence does not come from 'stranger danger' but from men they know." (Lori Heise, Co-director of the Center for the Health and Gender Equity.)
- At least one of every three women has been beaten, coerced into sex, or otherwise abused in her lifetime-(John Hopkins School of Health and Center for Health and Gender Equity)-

- Nearly one million cases of intimate partner violence are reported in America each year (Dept. of Justice with female victims outnumbering male victims by more than 5 to 1.
- There is a widely accepted estimate that 95% of those batterers are men.

- More that 1500 American women are killed by their husband or boyfriend every year, other references indicated 4000.
- According to domestic violence professional, Barbara Hart, battered women seek medical attention for injuries sustained more often after separation and 75% of ER visits for battered women occur after separation.
- 75% of the calls to law enforcement for intervention and assistance for domestic violence occur after separation.
- "Separation assault" is the attack on the women's body and violation in which her partner seeks to prevent her from leaving, retaliate for the separation, or force her to return. The force is to overbear her will so that he may manipulate where and whom we will live, and coercing her in order to enforce connection in a relationship.
- Ironically, a sizeable proportion of women are killed because they have made genuine efforts to leave their relationships, which have notably long histories of violence and abuse.
- Battered women often develop skills of survival rather than escape.

This statistical list could trail onto infinity. Some of these facts were perhaps already mentioned in earlier chaptersand others are just good food for thought to reveal the scope of this problem in our country.

Many women and children remain stuck in domestic violence for years because of the long list of risks to them if they try to leave. Some women do not know how to get out safely.

Some have given up trying-"learned helplessness".

Others, after many years of planning, found their way out of violence. There are a number of others who waited too long and have only books to record or news testimonies to bear witness to the details of their poor victims life:

- Locally, (front page story) estranged husband shot his wife who had left him and was battling in court to get away and stay away from the long history of violence. The estranged husband's father thought he was doing the abuser a favor by bailing him out of jail. The husband shot his wife, then shot himself, leaving three children without parents.
- Locally, (another front page) estranged husband shoots his wife, who had left him and the three children. He lived and went to prison.

This list also goes on and on.

We have talked about how the victim of violence comes to a wake up place while living this life of denial. The victims of domestic violence are awakened to what is really happening and the planning to escape can then begin. We will cover the escape plan at the end of this conclusion.

We reviewed what abuse was and how to determine the characteristics of the abuser. Much discussion has been shared about the impact on our emotions and how the concept of who we are is grossly impacted by living in this state of violence. The longer time spent in the violent environment, the worse the impact is on the women and children.

In earlier chapters we have also reviewed the importance of educational, proactive approaches to policy in various agencies in order to stop the cycle of violence in the homes of our children and grandchildren.

I want to thank you for allowing me to share some of the personal accounts of the life that my children and I had to endure until we found our way out of the violence. This book also stressed that there is a spiritual impact on a person's life when they have survived abuse. There is a correlation with perpetuating the cycles of abuse (i.e. may choose other abusive partners unless delivered and healed). You must get rid of past baggage close all spiritual doors that had been opened to spirits of violence, abuse, fear, rage, anger, bitterness, etc.

Ultimately, God's first and best choice for a man and his wife would be to work out their problems in love. When that same marriage adds "abuse" to the picture, it is no longer God's covenant that is being honored and upheld. When women and children and being emotionally damaged, physically, mentally, and sexually abused, women must find a safe way out as soon as all supports for her are lined up.

God does not want you to live like this!!! My advice is to get out of the marriage completely. Sever the abuse once and for all. Surely God can work miracles and do anything, but you should by no means risk your life or your children's lives while you wait for your miracle. Get out as soon as you safely can.

After the divorce, God can and does work miracles, but as noted earlier in Chapter 5, do not be deceived. Much fruit must be consistently seen for a long time before you should ever consider going back.

God wants us to have life and that more abundantly. In my situation, there was no fruit consistently for 17 years, yet there were many years of destruction and emotional stress and anguish. My marriage is over. There will be no reconciliation. That is not to say that God may not move differently in other people's situations, but NEVER live in violence no matter what! There is no justification for any violent behavior. A breakthrough can come for you and a plan of escape can be developed.

There are exhaustive resource lists for coalitions against domestic violence available in libraries nationwide. It is advisable to utilize only those resource lists that are most current. It was my experience while I researched for this book that many nationally listed addresses and phone numbers were outdated. I feel it is most effective to simply list the national domestic violence hotline which is equipped to connect any woman who is in distress with all local shelters hotline numbers for counseling, and human and social service in their home area that would be of service to them.

AND THE POWER AND GLORY FOREVER, AMEN.

Naturally, even a state or national number may at some point change currently The National Domestic Violence Hotline # is 1-800-799-7233.

If you are in an emergency that is life threatening and can't locate the number you can call 911 to get in touch with your local law enforcement agency.

When considering your plan of escape, I thought that one of the best examples of a personalized safety plan was developed by New York State Office for the Prevention of Domestic Violence, Charlotte Watson, Executive Director. This is a great plan that I want to print in this last section as written in *Finding Safety and Support, Domestic Violence Handbook*

If you have been candid with yourself and have come to a place where it is clear that you are living in a domestic violence situation, you should take the time to draw up your own safety plan. Just follow this format.

Personal Safety Plan: Being Ready For A Crisis

I can get help
- I can tell _____ about the violence and request they call the police if the hear noises coming from my house.
- I can teach my children how to contact the police. I will make sure they know our address and telephone number.

- If I have a programmable phone, I can program emergency numbers and teach my children how to use the autodial.
- I can teach my children how to go to _____ (i.e. neighbor's or business, etc.) for help if it is not possible to use the phone.

I can use my judgment

- When I expect my partner and I are going to argue, I will try to move to a space that is low risk, such as _____. (Try to avoid arguments in the bathroom, garage, kitchen, near a weapon, or in rooms without an outside exit.)
- I can also teach some of those strategies to some/ all of my children, as appropriate.

I can leave

If I decide to leave, I will _____
_____
_____
_____

(Practice how to get out safely. Write down your plan. What doors, windows, elevators, stairwells, or fire escapes would you use?)

- I can keep my purse and car keys ready and put them _____ in order to leave quickly.
- I will leave money and an extra set of keys with _____ so I can leave quickly.
- I will keep important documents at

  _____.
- If I have to leave my home, I will go to

  _____. If I cannot go to the above location, I can go to

  _____.

- The Domestic Violence Hotline Number is

  _____. I can call it if I need shelter or information.
- If it isn't safe to talk openly, I will use

  _____ as the code word/signal to my children that we are going to go, or to my family or friends we are coming.
- I will use _____ as my code word with my children or my friends so they will call for help.

Planning to Leave

- I will call a domestic violence program and get help making my plans. The hotline number for the nearest program is

  _____.

- I will leave money and an extra set of keys with_____ so I can leave quickly.
- I will keep copies of important documents or keys with _____. (E.g. children's birth certificates, you own personal titles, deeds, checks, copies of orders of protection, etc.)
- I can leave extra clothes with

    _____.
- I will keep important numbers and change for phone calls with me at all times. Since my partner can learn who I've been talking to by looking at phone bills, I can see if friends would let me use their phones and/or the phone credit cards.
- I can leave my pets with

    _____.
- I will check with _____ and _____ to see who would be able to let me stay with them or lend my some money.
- I can increase my independence by opening a bank account and getting credit cards in my own name, taking classes or getting job skills, getting copies of all the important papers and documents I might need and keeping them with _____.

- Other things I can do to increase my independence include:

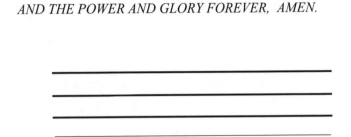

After I leave

- I can change the locks on my doors and windows.
- I can replace wooden doors with steel doors.
- I can install security systems including additional locks, window bars, poles to wedge against the door, and electronic system, etc.
- I can purchase rope ladders to be used for escape from second floor windows.
- I can install smoke detectors and put fire extinguishers on each floor in my home.
- I will teach my children how to use the phone to make a collect call to me if they are concerned about their safety.
- I will give the people who take care of my children, including their school, copies of custody and protective orders, and emergency phone numbers.

At work and in public

- I can inform my boss, the security supervisor and/or the employee assistance

program about my situation. The workplace
E.A.P. # is _____.

- My work place security office # is

    _____.

- I can ask _____ to screen
  my calls at work.

- When leaving work, I can

    _____

    _____.

- When traveling to and from work, I can vary
  my route. If there's trouble, I can

    _____

    _____.

- I can change my patterns. Avoid stores,
  banks, doctors appointments, Laundromats
  and

    _____

    places where my partner abuser might find
    me.

- I can tell _____ and
    _____ that I am
    no longer with my partner and ask them to
    call the police if they believe my children or
    myself are in danger.

AND THE POWER AND GLORY FOREVER, AMEN.

With an order of protection
- I will keep my order of protection

_____

.

Always keep it near you or your person.
- I will give copies of my order of protection to police departments in the community in which I live and those where I visit friends and family.
- I will give copies to my employer, my religious advisor, my closest friend, my children's school, day-care center and

_____.

- If my partner or abuse destroys my order of protection, or if I lose it, I can get another copy from the court that issued it.
- If my partner violates the order of protection, I can call the police and report a violation, contact my attorney, call my advocate, and and/or advise the court of the violation.
- I can call a domestic violence program if I have questions about how to enforce a court order or if I have problems getting it enforced.

I would like to interject a couple of points of my own here. If you would like to become proactive about your rights for better, self-advocacy on violence against women, you may get legal information from your local District Attorney's office and local library or log on to

You may request a copy of the Violence Against Women's Act passed in 1994 also, from your local D.A.'s office. The Violence Against Women Act states that domestic violence is a violation of a woman's civil rights. It also clearly states that a victim of domestic violence is entitled to obtain:
1. A civil court order of protection
2. A criminal court order of protection
3. A supreme court order of protection
The importance of obtaining more than one order of protection can only be realized given the need and dependent on how grueling the court battle has become.

In my situation, having both civil and criminal orders of protection assisted me in maintaining the supervised visitation, which protected my family from our abuser from coming back and forcing himself on all of us.

Items to take when leaving

- Identification of myself
- Children's birth certificates
- My birth certificate
- Social security cards
- School/vaccination records

- Money, checkbook, bank books, ATM cards, fax return
- Credit cards
- Medication
- Keys- house, car, office
- Driver's license, car registration
- Insurance papers
- Public Assistance ID / Medicaid cards (Related to this, the last heat, electric, phone, housing, and medical bills.)
- Passport, green card, working permit
- Divorce or separation papers
- Lease, rental agreement or house deed
- Car/mortgage payment book
- Children's toys, security blankets, stuffed animals
- Sentimental items, photos
- My personal safety plan

My Emotional Health

- If I am feeling down, lonely or confused, I can call _____ or the domestic violence hotline at
  _____.

- I can take care of my physical health needs by getting a check-up with my doctor, gynecologist and dentist. If I don't have a doctor, I will call a local clinic or _____ to get one.

- If I have concerns about my children's health and well being, I can call

  _____.

- If I have left my partner and am considering returning, I will call

  _____ or spend time with _____ before I make a decision.

- I will remind myself daily of my best qualities. They are: _____

  _____

  _____

  _____

  _____

- I can attend support groups, workshops, or classes at the local domestic violence program, or _____ in order to build a support system, learn skills or get information.

- I will look at how and when I drink alcohol or use other drugs (If I do).

- If I need help around my drinking or drug use, I can call _____.

- I can read one or more of the books listed in this books' bibliography that were written for battered women.

- Other things I can do to feel stronger are:

  _____
  _____
  _____
  _____

The above safety plan was developed by a group of domestic violence experts as a collaborative effort of the New York State Office for the Prevention of Domestic Violence (NYSOPDV)

Capital View Office Park

52 Washington St.

Rensselaer, NY 12144

This safety plan is a tool to assist you and it may be safer for you to work with an advocate and have someone you trust keep the personalized plan for you.

Please pray this prayer with me:

My Heavenly Father, Thank You for forgiving me of all sin.

Thank You for sending Your precious Son Jesus to die for me so that I may have eternal life.

AND THE POWER AND GLORY FOREVER, AMEN.

Jesus, thank You for being the Lord of my life, the strength of my life, and the love of my life.

Thank you for sending me Your Holy Spirit to comfort and keep me strong and directed.

Thank You so much for delivering me and my children out of a pit of violence.

Thank You that we are free of every threat and free of fear.

Thank You that we need not fear for you will send your angels to be in charge over us.

Thank You for placing a spiritual, mental, emotional, moral, physical, and financial hedge of protection over my children and myself.

Thank You, God, that with Your help I truly learn to walk with a full assurance that "No weapon formed against me shall prosper!"

In Jesus precious name, Amen.

AND THE POWER AND GLORY FOREVER, AMEN.

EPILOGUE

Suddenly, the field of darkness that I had fallen into burst into glorious light. There was **no more darkness**.

I began to see who I was, where I was going and what the Lord wanted me to do with my newfound freedom. The razor-sharp tendrils that bound me, or so I thought; dropped to the ground as I chose to **stand up**.

There was nothing left to bind me to immobility as long as I chose to continue to stand. I'm standing every day, and I remain standing.

No more fear–if fear comes to grip me, I run to my Father of light, my Lord Jesus Christ…

"No weapon formed against me shall prosper; every tongue that shall rise against me in judgment thou shalt condemn. This is the heritage of the servants of the Lord, and their righteousness is of Me, saith the Lord."

ISAIAH 54:17

REFERENCES

Arbitrell, Bowker and McFerron, Carlson B.E.
Children's Observations Of Inter-parental
Violence in Edwards, Battered Women and
Their Families

Battered Women. Greenhaven Press, San Diego,
CA. 1999

Berry, Dawn Bradley. Domestic Violence
Sourcebook. RGA Publishing Group, 1995

Brewster, Susan. To Be An Anchor in the Storm:
A Guide to Families. 1997

Brinegar, Jerry Lee. Breaking Free From Domestic
Violence. Minneapolis, MN Comp. Care
Publishers. 1992

Buzawa, Eve S. and Carl. Domestic Violence: The
Changing Criminal Justice Response.
Greenwood Publishing Group, Inc. 1992

Caldwell, Louis O. Beyond Guilt, a self-help book,
1980

Deluth. Power and Control Equality, DV Coalition,
printout

Domestic Violence Handbook (sound recording). The Coalition, Albany 1999

Evans, Patricia. Verbal Abuse Survivors Speak Out on Relationships and Recovery. Adams, Inc. Publishing Handbook, Mass. 1993

Havelin, Kate. My Parents Hurt Each Other: Family Violence. Capstone Press, Mankato MN

Jaffe, Wolfe and Wilson. Children of Battered Women. 1990

Jones, Ann. Next Time, She'll Be Dead: Battering and How to Stop It. Boston, Beacon Press, 1994

Kosof, Anna. Battered Women: Living With the Enemy. Franklin Watts, NY 1994

La Violette, Alyce D. It could happen to anyone: Why Battered Women Stay. Sage Publications, Oaks, CA 2000

Lissette, Andrea. Free Yourself From an Abusive Relationship (7 steps to getting free) Hunter House, Alameda, Ca. 2000

McCue, Marge Laird. Domestic Violence, pp. 83, 84. 1995

Morrison, Jan. A Safe Place. Harold Shaw Publishers, Wheaton Ill. 1990

Nelson, Noelle. Dangerous Relationships. How to Stop Domestic Violence Before it Stops You. Insight Books. 1997

NiCarthy, Ginny. The ones who got away. Women Who Left Abusive Partners. Seattle, The Seal Press, 1982

NiCarthy, Ginny. You Can Be Free. Seattle, The Seal Press, 1989

NiCarthy, Ginny. Getting Free: A Handbood for Women in Abusive Relationships. Seattle, The Seal Press, 1982

Parrot, Andrea. Coping With Date Rape & Acquaintance Rape. Rosen Publishing Group, New York. 1993

Shelman, Eric A. Out of the Darkness: The Story of Mary Ellen Wilson. Dolphin Moon Publishing, Lake Forest, CA. 1998

Steinman, Michael. Woman Battering: Policy Responses. University of Nebraska, Lincoln 1991

Strauss, M.A. and Gilles R. J. Physical Violence In
    American Families

Thornhill, R. and Palmer, Craig T. Rape:
    Biological Basis of Sexual Coercion. 2000

Walker, Lenore. "The Battered Woman" 1979

Wilkerson, Dave. Pulpit series Newsletter: The
    Measured Glory of God. Times square
    church, 2000

Winkler, Kathleen. Date Rape. A Hot Issue.
    Ensloe Publishers, Inc.

Zeineit, Karen. Victims of Teen Violence.
    Ensloe Publishers, Inc. 1996